Building a Home Security System with Raspberry Pi

Build your own sophisticated modular home security system using the popular Raspberry Pi board

Matthew Poole

BIRMINGHAM - MUMBAI

Building a Home Security System with Raspberry Pi

First published: December 2015

Production reference: 1161215

Published by Packt Publishing Ltd.
Livery Place
35 Livery Street
Birmingham B3 2PB, UK.

ISBN 978-1-78217-527-8

www.packtpub.com

Credits

Author
Matthew Poole

Reviewers
Lihang Li
Cédric Verstraeten

Commissioning Editor
Edward Bowkett

Acquisition Editors
Vivek Anantharaman
Vinay Argekar

Content Development Editor
Sumeet Sawant

Technical Editor
Namrata Patil

Copy Editor
Angad Singh

Project Coordinator
Shweta H. Birwatkar

Proofreader
Safis Editing

Indexer
Rekha Nair

Production Coordinator
Manu Joseph

Cover Work
Manu Joseph

About the Author

Matthew Poole is a systems engineer based near Southampton on the south coast of England with over 20 years of industry experience. After graduating in electronics and communications engineering, he went on to train as and to become an air traffic engineer for the UK Civil Aviation Authority, working on microprocessor-based control and communications systems.

Later, he became a software architect and mobile technology specialist, and worked for several consultancies and global organizations. He is now a partner at UK Mobile Media, a boutique systems consultancy focused on designing Bluetooth and other wireless systems, taking ideas from concept to prototype. He is also the director of technology for Mobile Onboard, a leading UK-based transport technology company that specializes in on-bus connectivity and mobile ticketing.

About the Reviewers

Lihang Li received his MS degree in computer vision from National Laboratory of Pattern Recognition(NLPR) at Institute of Automation of the Chinese Academy of Sciences (CAS). His interests include Linux, open source, cloud computing, virtualization, computer vision algorithms, machine learning and data mining, and a variety of programming languages.

You can find him at his personal website at `http://hustcalm.me`.

> It has been a great opportunity being a part of this book. I have always been a fan of embedded devices and systems. Thanks go to our author and coordinator. Hope the readers will find this book helpful.

Cédric Verstraeten has an MSc in engineering and is primarily active in the C++ community. He works as a software engineer and is a huge open source enthusiast. He spends most of his time on side projects. He's the founder of Kerberos.io, an open source video surveillance system built for the Raspberry Pi, and is the organizer of the Raspberry Pi Belgium meetup group.

> I would like to thank Packt Publishing for making me a reviewer of this book. I really think their books can give people an in-depth overview of a particular topic.

www.PacktPub.com

Support files, eBooks, discount offers, and more

For support files and downloads related to your book, please visit www.PacktPub.com.

Did you know that Packt offers eBook versions of every book published, with PDF and ePub files available? You can upgrade to the eBook version at www.PacktPub.com and as a print book customer, you are entitled to a discount on the eBook copy. Get in touch with us at service@packtpub.com for more details.

At www.PacktPub.com, you can also read a collection of free technical articles, sign up for a range of free newsletters and receive exclusive discounts and offers on Packt books and eBooks.

https://www2.packtpub.com/books/subscription/packtlib

Do you need instant solutions to your IT questions? PacktLib is Packt's online digital book library. Here, you can search, access, and read Packt's entire library of books.

Why subscribe?

- Fully searchable across every book published by Packt
- Copy and paste, print, and bookmark content
- On demand and accessible via a web browser

Free access for Packt account holders

If you have an account with Packt at www.PacktPub.com, you can use this to access PacktLib today and view 9 entirely free books. Simply use your login credentials for immediate access.

Table of Contents

Preface

The Raspberry Pi is a powerful, low-cost, credit-card sized computer, which lends itself perfectly as the controller of a sophisticated home security system. Using the available on-board interfaces, the Raspberry Pi can be expanded to allow the connection of a virtually infinite number of security sensors and devices. The Raspberry Pi has the processing power and interfaces available to build a sophisticated home security system but at a fraction of the cost of commercially available systems.

Building a Home Security System with Raspberry Pi starts off by showing you the Raspberry Pi and how to set up the Linux-based operating system. The book then guides you through connecting switch sensors and LEDs to the native GPIO connector safely, and it also shows you how to access these using simple Bash scripts. As you dive further in, you'll learn how to build an input/output expansion board using the I2C interface and power supply, allowing the connection of the large number of sensors needed for a typical home security setup.

The book features clear diagrams and code listing every step of the way to allow you to build a truly sophisticated and modular home security system.

What this book covers

Chapter 1, Setting Up Your Raspberry Pi, starts out by taking our Raspberry Pi out of its box and preparing it for being the centerpiece of our home security system. Along the way, we will install and set up the operating system, connect our Pi to the network, and access it remotely. We'll also secure our Pi and make sure it can keep the right time.

Chapter 2, Connecting Things to Your Pi with GPIO, explores the GPIO port and the various interfaces it features. We'll look at the various things we can connect to the Raspberry Pi using the GPIO including switches and sensors as we start to build our home security system.

Chapter 3, Extending Your Pi to Connect More Things, looks at ways of expanding the number of things we can connect to our Raspberry Pi, overcoming the limitation of having just the eight digital pins available to us on the GPIO by tapping into other interfaces on the GPIO and building our own input/output expansion board.

Chapter 4, Adding a Magnetic Contact Sensor, starts to actually connect things to our home security system, such as magnetic sensors and other types of contact devices. You will learn how to program our I2C expansion port using Bash scripts so that we can read the state of our sensors and switch on warning LEDs. We'll also start to develop the control scripts for our system that will allow us to arm and disarm the system and add delay timers.

Chapter 5, Adding a Passive Infrared Motion Sensor, looks at passive infra-red motion detectors, how they work, and how we can connect wired and wireless types to our home security system. We'll also learn how to create log files based on events using Bash scripts so that we can maintain a history of detector states as they change.

Chapter 6, Adding Cameras to Our Security System, teaches you how to connect both Raspberry Pi camera modules and USB cameras to our Pi board in order to take image and video captures when required by our home security system. We'll also learn how to overlay our images with informative text and have the files immediately emailed to us.

Chapter 7, Building a Web-Based Control Panel, gets down to the business of starting to put together modules by building a mobile-optimized web-based control panel for our home security system. You'll learn how to set up a web server on our Raspberry Pi and manipulate files using our web control panel, meaning we'll start to explore how all of the elements so far will come together as part of our final system.

Chapter 8, A Miscellany of Things, looks a few other bits and pieces, such as adding other sensors to our home security system that are not necessarily related to intruder detection. We'll also look at how we can administer our entire Raspberry Pi system remotely using a web browser in addition to accessing our home security control panel.

Chapter 9, Putting It All Together, is the moment we've all been waiting for; we're going to take all of the elements and concepts from the previous chapters and put together our full system comprising the elements we want to feature. The star of the show will be our Bash scripts, which will glue together all of these elements and provide the control logic for the entire system.

What you need for this book

You'll need the following software:

- Gparted dd fake-hwclock
- Win32 Disk Imager 0.9.5 PuTTY
- i2c-tools

Who this book is for

This book is for anyone who is interested in building a modular home security system from scratch using a Raspberry Pi board, basic electronics, sensors, and simple scripts. This book is ideal for enthusiastic novice programmers, electronics hobbyists, and engineering professionals. It would be great if you have some basic soldering skills in order to build some of the interface modules.

Conventions

In this book, you will find a number of styles of text that distinguish between different kinds of information. Here are some examples of these styles, and an explanation of their meaning.

Code words in text, database table names, folder names, filenames, file extensions, pathnames, dummy URLs, user input, and Twitter handles are shown as follows: "Extract 2015-09-24-raspbian-jessie.img to your Home folder."

A block of code is set as follows:

```
# passwd
root@raspberrypi:/home/pi# passwd
Enter new UNIX password:
Retype new UNIX password:
passwd: password updated successfully
root@raspberrypi:/home/pi#
```

Any command-line input or output is written as follows:

```
$ sudo apt-get install fake-hwclock
```

New terms and **important words** are shown in bold. Words that you see on the screen, in menus or dialog boxes for example, appear in the text like this: "Type the IP address of the Raspberry Pi into the Host Name box and click on **Open**."

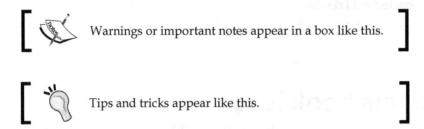

> Warnings or important notes appear in a box like this.

> Tips and tricks appear like this.

Reader feedback

Feedback from our readers is always welcome. Let us know what you think about this book—what you liked or may have disliked. Reader feedback is important for us to develop titles that you really get the most out of.

To send us general feedback, simply send an e-mail to feedback@packtpub.com, and mention the book title via the subject of your message.

If there is a topic that you have expertise in and you are interested in either writing or contributing to a book, see our author guide on www.packtpub.com/authors.

Customer support

Now that you are the proud owner of a Packt book, we have a number of things to help you to get the most from your purchase.

Downloading the example code

You can download the example code files for all Packt books you have purchased from your account at http://www.packtpub.com. If you purchased this book elsewhere, you can visit http://www.packtpub.com/support and register to have the files e-mailed directly to you.

Errata

Although we have taken every care to ensure the accuracy of our content, mistakes do happen. If you find a mistake in one of our books—maybe a mistake in the text or the code—we would be grateful if you could report this to us. By doing so, you can save other readers from frustration and help us improve subsequent versions of this book. If you find any errata, please report them by visiting http://www.packtpub.com/submit-errata, selecting your book, clicking on the Errata Submission Form link, and entering the details of your errata. Once your errata are verified, your submission will be accepted and the errata will be uploaded to our website or added to any list of existing errata under the Errata section of that title.

To view the previously submitted errata, go to https://www.packtpub.com/books/content/support and enter the name of the book in the search field. The required information will appear under the Errata section.

Piracy

Piracy of copyright material on the Internet is an ongoing problem across all media. At Packt, we take the protection of our copyright and licenses very seriously. If you come across any illegal copies of our works, in any form, on the Internet, please provide us with the location address or website name immediately so that we can pursue a remedy.

Please contact us at copyright@packtpub.com with a link to the suspected pirated material.

We appreciate your help in protecting our authors, and our ability to bring you valuable content.

Questions

You can contact us at questions@packtpub.com if you are having a problem with any aspect of the book, and we will do our best to address it.

1
Setting Up Your Raspberry Pi

Before we can get into the realms of building our home security system, there's a bit of preparation work needed to get our Raspberry Pi up and running. So, we're going to go through the initial steps needed to get our Pi ready to be worked on.

In this chapter, we will cover the following topics:

- Exploring the different versions of the Raspberry Pi that are available
- Choosing the right Raspberry Pi version for your system
- Preparing the SD Card with the Raspbian Operating System
- Learning how to remotely access the Raspberry Pi over your home network
- Updating our operating system with the latest packages
- Exploring the time-keeping options on the Raspberry Pi
- Setting the user and root passwords to secure our Raspberry Pi

Which flavor of Pi?

Since the Raspberry Pi was released in 2012, there have been several versions of the mini-PC board released. I'll go though each of the versions released with their respective features so that you can choose which one is suitable for your particular project.

The good news is that it doesn't really matter which version you use in terms of power, as our home security system doesn't necessarily need loads of processing power, depending on what you want your system to do, of course). You might have an older board kicking about that will work for you.

The other piece of good news is that the GPIO interface pin layouts are the same across all the versions. The later versions have more pins, but the original 26 pins still remain in the same place.

The latest Raspberry Pi Version 2

Raspberry Pi Model A

The baby of the family is the Model A; it was released as a lower-cost version of the Model B, shown in the following section. Its main differences from the Model B are that it features just 256Mb of memory and has no Ethernet port; so if you want to connect this board to a network, you are limited to using a USB Wi-Fi dongle.

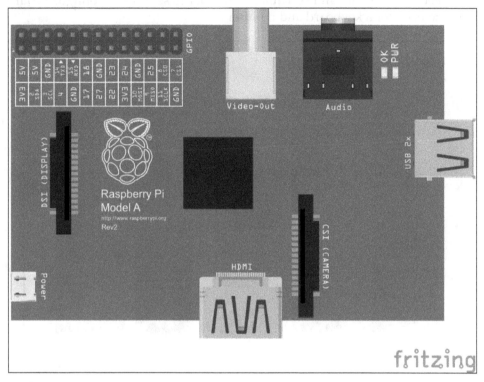

The Raspberry Pi Model A Board Layout

Raspberry Pi Model B

This was the first version of Raspberry Pi to be released; an updated revision, which improved the power system and USB port protection, came later. It features 512Mb of memory and has an Ethernet port for connecting to your network. This is probably the most common version used, and having the Ethernet port is incredibly useful, especially to get up and run quickly in order to set up and configure your Pi without the need for a keyboard and monitor.

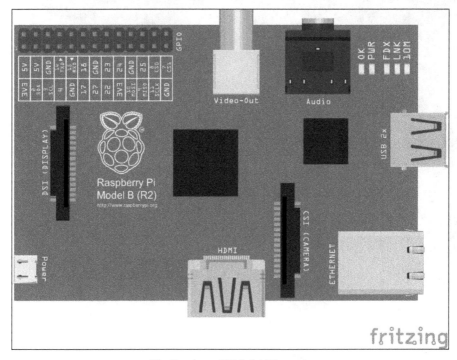

The Raspberry Pi Model B Layout

Raspberry Pi Model B+ and Model 2

In 2014, the Raspberry Pi Foundation released a new version of the board that had some fundamental changes as compared to the previous version. The most fundamental changes were the board layout, form factor, and mounting points—much to the dismay of the many enclosure and accessory manufacturers out there.

In fact, we were in the middle of prototyping an enclosure for a commercial product that we were developing based on the Raspberry Pi—fortunately we caught wind of the board change in the nick of time and were able to change our enclosure to support the upcoming model B+.

The main electronic changes to this board are the addition of 2 more USB ports that can deliver more power to peripherals, an expanded GPIO interface, and the removal of the composite video port that is now consolidated into the audio jack. It also now uses a micro SD card with a better card slot.

In February 2015, a more powerful Raspberry Pi was released: the Raspberry Pi Model 2. It's similar to the Model B+ in terms of form-factor and interfaces, but is now reportedly 6-times faster than the Model B/B+ with its upgraded ARM processor and 1Gb of memory.

At the same low cost of less than £30, it's a fantastic little board and a great power-house for embedded systems.

The Raspberry Pi Model B+ and Model 2 Layout

Model comparison table

	Model A	Model B	Model B+	Version 2
Processor	ARM1176JZF-S 700 MHz processor, VideoCore IV GPU			Quad-core ARM Cortex-A7 CPU and a VideoCore IV dual-core GPU
Memory	256Kb	512Kb	512Kb	1Gb
USB Ports	2	2	4	4

	Model A	Model B	Model B+	Version 2
Ethernet	No	Yes	Yes	Yes
No.GPIO Pins	26	26	40	40
Storage	SD Card	SD Card	Micro SD Card	Micro SD Card

So which one?

Essentially, any version of the Raspberry Pi will work with the modules presented in this book, but if you want to exploit features such as the camera, which may require more processing power and memory, or want to have an Ethernet connection, you'll need to use the Model B.

If you want to start plugging additional stuff into the USB port, such as a GSM modem, then I recommend that you use the Model B+ as it delivers more power to those kinds of devices without the need for additional USB hubs.

If you want to do more processing with video and images from an attached camera, or want to connect lots of things, then go for the latest **Model 2** board. I'm going to assume that's the one you have chosen for this project, and that's the one I'll be using throughout this book; just be aware of any limitations if you choose to use an earlier model.

 The Raspberry Pi Foundation site has more detailed information about each model. You can visit it at https://www.raspberrypi.org/products.

Preparing the SD card

The Raspberry Pi only boots from an SD card (or micro SD card for the B+ and v2 models), and cannot boot from an external drive or USB stick (well that's not strictly true, but is beyond the scope of this book).

It's recommended that you use a Class 10 SD card for performance, but a Class 4 or 6 card will be fine for this project. You'll need to have a minimum card size of 4Gb.

Now that we have our Raspberry Pi board and SD card to hand, we need to prepare the SD Card specifically for our home security system. We're going to use the standard Raspbian operating system as there really is no reason to use any other distribution; it's the de facto choice for the Raspberry Pi.

Downloading the Raspbian image

You'll need to grab the latest **Raspbian OS** image from the Raspberry Pi site at https://www.raspberrypi.org/downloads.

Download the Raspbian OS ZIP file containing the image to your PC.

 At the time of writing, the latest version was Raspbian Jessie version 4.1 (2015-09-24-raspbian-jessie.zip).

Once downloaded, unzip the file and you'll have the file, 2015-09-24-raspbian-jessie.img.

The next thing to do is burn this image to your SD card...

Using Microsoft Windows

On a Windows PC, the best way to burn the image to your SD card is to use the **Win32 Disk Imager** utility. This can be downloaded from http://sourceforge.net/projects/win32diskimager.

 The current version, at the time of writing, is 0.9.5.

It doesn't have an installer, and launches directly from the EXE file.

Now, it's time to create your SD card image:

1. Insert your SD card into the PC and launch the Win32 Disk Imager.
2. Select the SD card device drive letter (make sure it's right!).
3. Choose the Raspbian image file you've just downloaded.

4. Click on the **Write** button to create the SD card image.

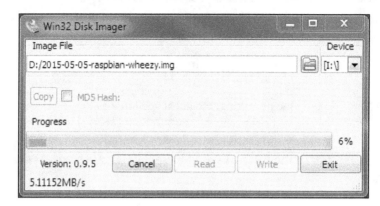

Using Linux

On a Linux PC, you'll need to use the **gparted** and **dd** utilities to burn the image on your SD card.

Carry out the following steps to create your SD card image:

1. Extract `2015-09-24-raspbian-jessie.img` to your `Home` folder.

2. Insert your SD card into the PC.

3. If you're not already in a shell terminal window, open one (you can use *Ctrl + Alt + T* on most graphical-based desktop systems).

4. Type the following command in the shell terminal:

   ```
   $ sudo fdisk -l
   ```

   In the list check, your SD card appears as a drive device (for example, `/dev/sdb`). It's crucial that you ensure you use the right device in the next step. We'll assume that your device is `/sdb`.

5. To burn the image to the SD card, type the following command:

   ```
   $ sudo dd if=2015-09-24-raspbian-jessie.img of=/dev/sdb
   ```

6. Hit *Enter* and go make a cup of tea or coffee as this will take a while. You'll know that it's finished when the command ($) prompt re-appears.

7. When the command prompt does re-appear, type the following command:

   ```
   $ sudo sync
   ```

8. Once that command has finished, you can remove the SD card from the PC.

Booting your Pi

You're now ready to boot up your Raspberry Pi. Pop your shiny new SD card into it and plug in the power.

Assuming that you have a monitor attached to your Pi, you should see your system booting up nicely. Although you could wait for it to boot up and connect to it via a terminal session (we'll look at that later), I recommend that you connect a monitor to it, at least in the first instance, just to make sure everything is working correctly.

In the new **Jessie** version of Raspbian, you'll boot straight into a desktop GUI, which is a major change from previous versions, where you'd be taken to the **raspi-config** utility, the first time the system is run, where you'd set up your Pi, and importantly, expand the file system to use the entire space available on your SD card.

Debian Jessie boots into the GUI by default

Expanding the file system

When you first create your Raspbian SD card, you'll only be left with about 200Mb of space in the file system, regardless of the size of your SD card. This is not much use, so we want to expand the file system so that it uses all of the available space on the card.

Fortunately, this is very easy on the Raspberry Pi now, as this function is available in the Raspberry Pi Configuration Tool on the desktop.

To access the new configuration tool, go to **Menu** and select **Preferences |
Raspberry Pi Configuration**.

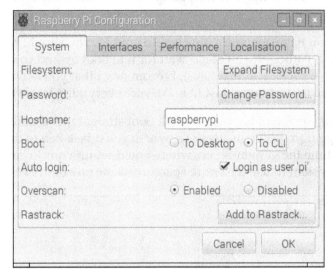

The new Raspberry Pi Configuration Tool

Goodbye GUI

Most of our work is going to be done in the command-line
interface (CLI). Therefore, before we reboot the system in a
minute, let's change the **Boot** option by selecting **To CLI**, as
shown in the previous screenshot, so boot into the command
line going forward.

Anyway, now we click on the **Expand Filesystem** button, and in a couple of seconds,
you'll see a confirmation message. The filesystem will be expanded when the system
next reboots.

Using the raspi-config utility

If you have an older version of Raspbian, or you're not using the desktop GUI, then
you'll need to use the raspi-config utility (which is still better than the old days when
we had to do this manually in the shell). The first time you boot up, you'll be taken
straight to the raspi-config utility.

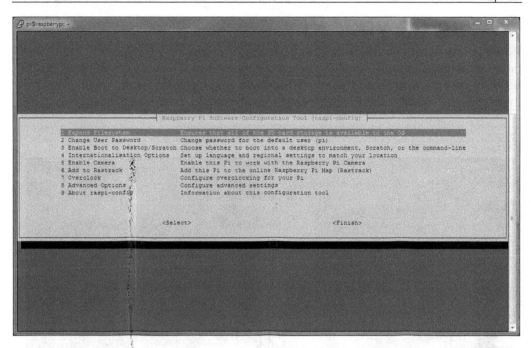

The first option is the Expand Filesystem option; select this and you'll see various commands scrolling up the screen. Once it's finished, you'll see the following message:

```
Root partition has been resized.
The filesystem will be enlarged upon the next reboot
```

Click on OK.

Select Finish on the config screen and reboot your Pi when prompted.

After your Pi reboots with its fuller file system, you'll be taken straight to the shell prompt where you can log in with the default user and password.

Login: pi

Password: raspberry

Setting up your Pi

When you boot into the shell and have the Ethernet connected, hopefully the Pi will have connected to your home network and acquired an IP address from your router. If this is the case, you should see the **IP address** that has been issued just before the login prompt, as shown in the following screenshot:

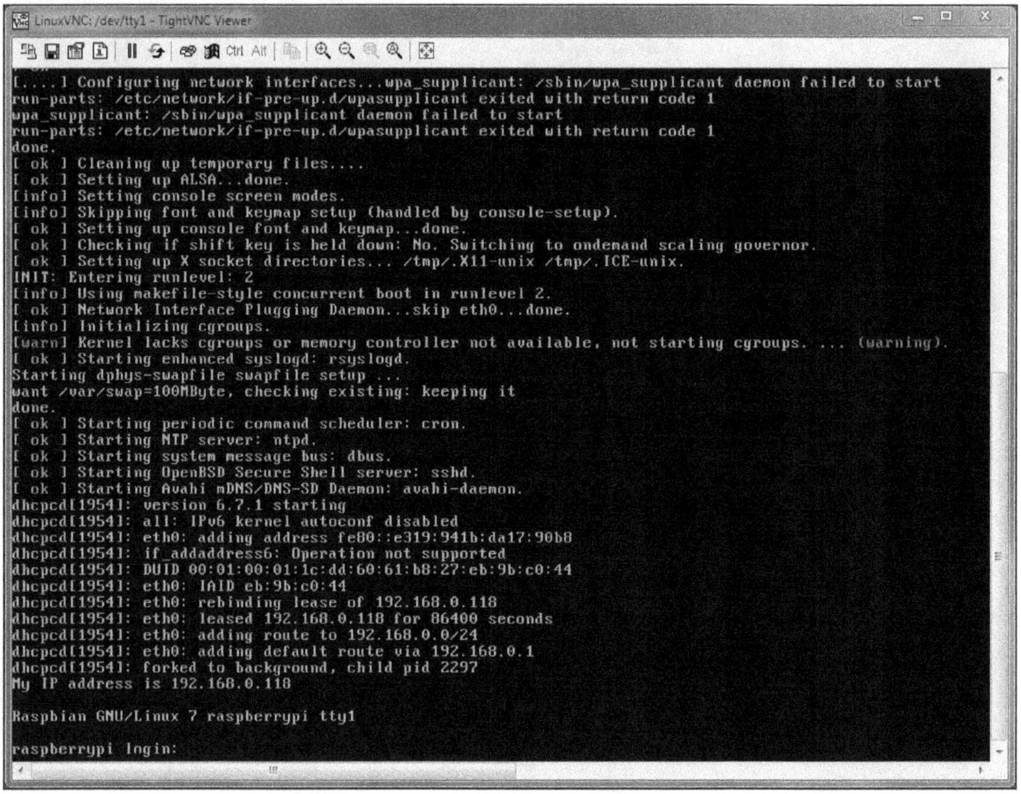

As you can see from my screenshot, it's given me the IP address, `192.168.0.118`. This is good because I can now access the Pi remotely, using a secure shell (SSH) client to connect to it from the comfort of my laptop. This is particularly useful when my Pi is in the office and I want to sit on my sofa in front of the telly but still work on it, which I often do when I'm feeling lazy.

Downloading the example code

You can download the example code files from your account at http://www.packtpub.com for all the Packt Publishing books you have purchased. If you purchased this book elsewhere, you can visit http://www.packtpub.com/support and register to have the files e-mailed directly to you.

To do this, download **PuTTY**: a utility that allows you to connect to shell terminals remotely over the network. You can download it from http://www.putty.org.

Install and launch **PuTTY** and you're ready to connect to your Pi remotely from the comfort of your sofa.

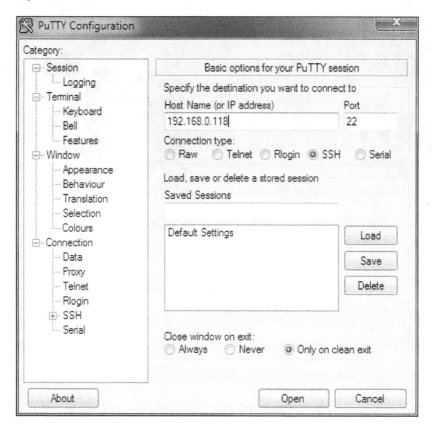

Type the IP address of the Raspberry Pi into the Host Name box and click on **Open**. You'll be connected to your Pi in a remote terminal window. Once you've logged in, you can do pretty much everything on your Pi, as if you were sitting in front of it.

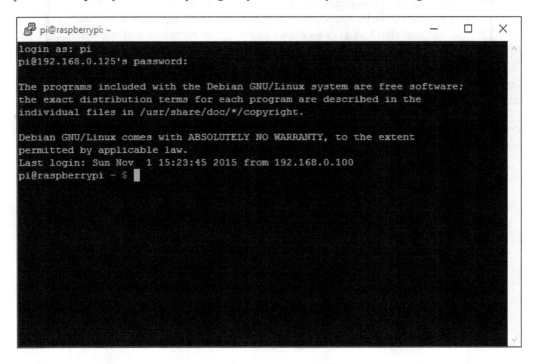

We'll assume from now on that most of the work we do will be through a remote shell session, unless highlighted otherwise.

If you want to use the command line to launch the Raspberry Pi remote shell — for example, from another Linux system — use the following command from your terminal window:

```
# ssh pi@192.168.0.125
```

You'll then be prompted for the Pi's password and taken into a shell session.

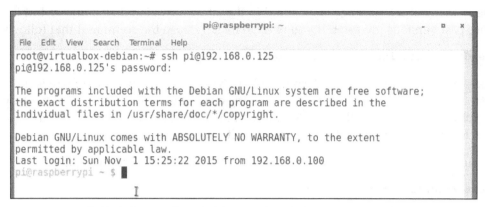

The Pi shell session launched from a Debian desktop terminal window

Getting up to date

Something that you should get into the habit of doing is updating the operating system regularly; even though you may have the latest image installed, it's very likely that there are updated packages available. To update your OS, enter the following command:

```
$ sudo apt-get update
```

After this, enter the following one:

```
$ sudo apt-get dist-upgrade
```

This may take a while, depending on the number of updates required.

Getting the right time

The Raspberry Pi doesn't have on-board real-time clock hardware. This is one of the deliberate omissions to keep the cost of the board down. Instead, the Pi gets its time when it boots up from time servers on the Internet using the **Network Time Protocol (NTP)**. However, if there is no Internet connection at the time of booting up, then the time will be wrong.

 In our security system, it's important that the time is kept accurate so that timestamps on log files and images are correct.

fake-hwclock

The `fake-hwclock` package is included in the latest Raspbian distributions, but in other past versions it wasn't. If you need to install it, use the command that follows:

```
$ sudo apt-get install fake-hwclock
```

`fake-hwclock` is used by the Raspberry Pi to try and keep time when there is no network connection. It will regularly save the current time and restore it at boot-up. The obvious problem with this is that if the Pi has been switched off a few days, then the time will be set to the last time that it was on, using `fake-hwclock`.

If you want to see what time it last logged, type the following command:

```
$ cat /etc/fake-hwclock.data
```

ntp

The **Network Time Protocol (NTP)** is used when there is an Internet connection available and it can request the latest most accurate time from one or more time servers on the Internet.

By default, the **ntp service** is enabled on the latest Raspbian distribution, but it will initially get its time at boot-up from `fake-hwclock` if there is no Internet connection. There may be times when it's necessary to force the ntp service to update from the Internet—for example, if the Internet connection is restored sometime after boot-up.

To force the ntp service to update from the Internet, use the following commands:

```
$ service ntp stop
$ ntpd -gq
$ service ntp start
```

Talking of security…

There's no point in having a security system if the system itself is not secure. So, now we'll change the default password for the **pi** user.

From the prompt, type the following command:

```
$ sudo passwd pi
pi@raspberrypi ~ $ sudo passwd pi
Enter new UNIX password:
Retype new UNIX password:
passwd: password updated successfully
```

What is this sudo thing anyway?

You'd have noticed that we've been putting sudo at the start of each command that we run in the terminal window. This is so that commands are run as the **root user** – the highest security level. This elevated security is required to perform many operations. sudo actually means *super do*.

If you can't be bothered to type sudo every time, then you can switch to the super user by typing the following:

```
$ sudo su
```

You'll see that the prompt changed from a $ to a #, which indicates that you are now running as the root user.

So, this might be a good time to change the root user password too! To do this, type the following:

```
# passwd
root@raspberrypi:/home/pi# passwd
Enter new UNIX password:
Retype new UNIX password:
passwd: password updated successfully
root@raspberrypi:/home/pi#
```

Connecting via Wi-Fi

You can also connect your Raspberry Pi to your network using Wi-Fi by plugging a USB dongle into it. There are additional configuration steps required to make this work, which are beyond the scope of this chapter, but there are many resources available covering this subject.

 You can find recipes for connecting your Raspberry Pi using Wi-Fi in the **Raspberry Pi Networking Cookbook** by Rick Golden, published by Packt Publishing (https://www.packtpub.com/hardware-and-creative/raspberry-pi-networking-cookbook).

Summary

In this chapter, we took our Raspberry Pi out of its box and prepared it to be the centerpiece of our home security system. Along the way, we installed and set up the operating system, connected our Pi to the network, and accessed it remotely. We also secured our Pi and made sure it could keep the right time.

In the next chapter, we're going to explore the GPIO port and the various interfaces it features. We'll look at the various things we can connect to the Raspberry Pi using the GPIO port, including switches and sensors, as we start to build our home security system.

2

Connecting Things to Your Pi with GPIO

The Raspberry Pi has lots of ways to connect things to it, such as plugging things into the USB ports, connecting devices to the on-board camera and display ports, and connecting things to the various interfaces that make up the **GPIO connector**. As part of our home security project, we'll be focusing mainly on connecting things to the GPIO connector.

In this chapter, we will cover the following topics:

- Examining the GPIO connector and what each of the pins does
- Learning about the I2C and SPI buses that will be used in later chapters
- Connecting an LED and a switch safely to the data pins, and accessing these data pins using simple scripts
- Understanding the USB ports and their limitations

Prerequisites

Along with your Raspberry Pi, you'll need the following parts for the projects in this chapter:

- A breadboard
- An LED
- A 220 ohm resistor (red, red, black)
- A 10K ohm resistor (brown, black, orange)
- A pushbutton or toggle switch

- A hook-up wire:

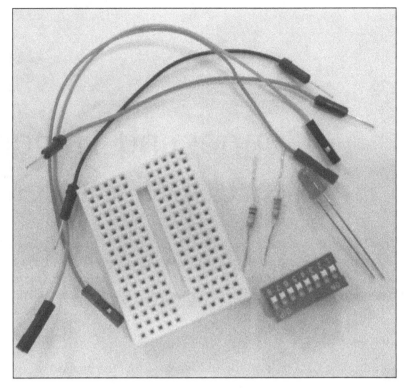

Our little collection of parts

Say hello to the GPIO

The GPIO connector is the large group of pins on the edge of your Raspberry Pi board. On earlier models, there were 26 pins that made up this connector. But, ever since the Model B+, there have been 40 pins, although the first 26 pins are identical to the previous models, and it's these 26 pins we'll be working with. You won't need to worry about the rest of the pins.

Essentially, the GPIO connector provides access to following:

- Power supplies
- Digital I/O pins
- I2C bus
- SPI bus
- UART Serial bus

Some of the pins on the GPIO have more than one purpose, depending on how they are programmed. The following diagram is a reference guide to all of the pins on the GPIO. The GPIO numbers on the yellow labels relate directly to those on the Broadcom chip, and are numbers generally used within the scripts.

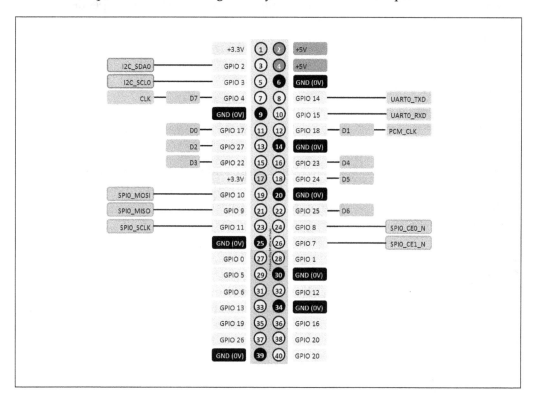

Digital I/O pins

The GPIO has 8 digital input/output pins available for use. These can be used to switch things on and off (in output mode), and also to detect when external things are switched on and off (input mode). Each pin can be configured independently for input or output operation, and I have labelled them **D0** to **D7** in the preceding diagram.

Obviously, if we were to use each of these pins to drive or sense an individual device, we would be limited to a maximum of 8 devices that could be connected to our home security system. In many scenarios, this is probably not enough, so in the next chapter we'll learn how to use the GPIO to connect many more things to our Raspberry Pi.

The I2C bus

The **Inter-Integrated Circuit (I2C)** bus is a low-speed interface that can connect multiple devices and simple sensors using a 2-wire interface without the need for a separate clock or device select line. Typically, this bus can operate at speeds up to 100kbit/s. We'll be covering this in the next chapter to help us expand our digital I/O and connect more things.

The SPI bus

The **Serial Peripheral Interface (SPI)** bus is a synchronous two-way serial connection between a master and a slave device. It can be used to access more complex sensors or drive displays.

The master device provides the synchronization, and each transmission is synchronized by a clock pulse on **SCLK** (GPIO11/pin 23). Data is transmitted on the **MOSI** (master-out-slave-in) and **MISO** (master-in-slave-out) (pins 19 and 21 respectively).

The UART serial bus

The **Universal Asynchronous Receiver and Transmitter (UART)** bus is a way to communicate with external devices over a serial data connection, and is a common way for the Raspberry Pi to access data from devices such as GPS modules, which often come with serial connections. It can be a little bit fiddly getting the Pi set up to communicate with UART-connected devices, as it's also tied in with the operating system's serial console.

USB ports

We're probably all familiar with **Universal Serial Bus (USB)** ports as we use them to connect all sorts of things to our PCs, such as keyboards, mouses, and hard disks. On the Raspberry Pi, it's just the same; we can connect keyboards, mouses, and dongles to give us Wi-Fi and Bluetooth connectivity.

Official Raspberry Pi USB Wi-Fi Dongle

On earlier Raspberry Pi models, the amount of current that the ports delivered was pretty low and caused all sorts of problems if too much current was drawn by the connected devices. This was significantly improved from the model B+ onwards, and it's now possible to connect GSM/LTE dongles without any problems.

There are still limitations, however, if you want to connect things such as hard disk drives; these can still draw more current than what can be supplied by the Raspberry Pi USB ports, so it's recommended that a powered USB hub or USB power injector be used when connecting these types of devices to your Pi.

Power connections

The GPIO connector also provides access to the on-board power supplies. The +5V connection (pins 2 and 4) is essentially the +5V input from the external power supply connected to the micro-USB power port. This can be used to power small external circuits if necessary, although it is recommended that an additional external +5V supply be used if significant current is required.

The +3.3V supply (pins 1 and 17) is the output from the on-board 3.3V regulator and provides a small amount of current up to 50mA. If you need to draw more than 50mA for your external circuits, then you should use an external power supply. I'll show you how to build one later in this book.

The I/O pins on the Raspberry Pi operate at 3.3V levels. Connecting voltages higher than this to the pins could irreversibly damage your Pi. If you follow the instructions in this book, then everything should be fine, but randomly connecting things to your Pi that use lots of power will break it!

Getting acquainted with the GPIO

Before we embark on connecting lots of things to our Pi board, it might be a good idea to just get acquainted with the GPIO through a couple of simple projects that will help us understand how to interact with the digital I/O pins using shell scripts.

Let there be light

This simple little project shows how to connect a GPIO output to an LED, and switch it on and off using shell commands.

The following diagram shows how to connect up the circuit using a breadboard:

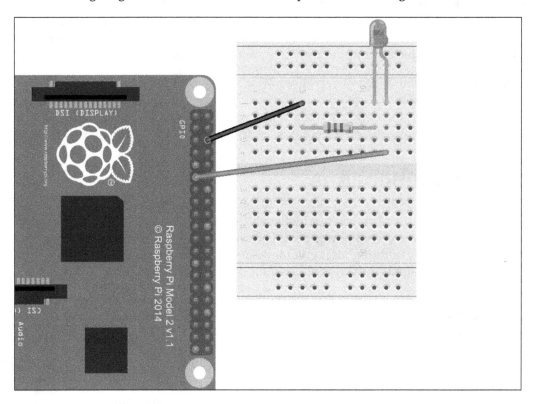

 The pretty diagram that you just saw was produced using a free software tool from fritzing, which is an open-source hardware initiative to make electronics accessible as creative material for anyone. Download it from fritzing.org.

The LED anode (the positive side) is connected to the **D0** digital I/O (pin 11 of the connector or GPIO17). When this pin is switched on, it will provide a 3.3V supply to the LED.

The LED is connected to the Ground pin via a 220R resistor on the cathode (negative side). The resistor limits the voltage to the LED and the current through it, otherwise it would burn out, as you can only supply up to about 2V to LEDs. With a current of around 10mA being drawn by the LED on a 3.3V supply, a 220R resistor works well to protect both it and the GPIO.

Here's the circuit diagram for it:

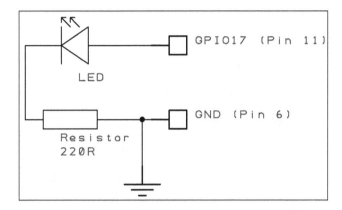

Calculating LED Resistor Values...

While this book is not really a course on electronics theory, I thought it would be handy to show you how to work out the resistor values for LEDs using Ohms Law, as we'll be covering this again later.

As I mentioned, a typical LED will drop about 2V across it, although this varies according to color and type. This is called the forward voltage of the device or VLED.

 The current required by an LED is around 10mA, again depending on its specification. We'll call this current flowing through the LED, ILED.

Essentially, the voltage across the resistor will be the supply voltage minus the voltage drop across the LED (for example,.2V). So, if we have a 12V supply (VS), the voltage across the resistor will be 10V (VS – VLED).

According to Ohms Law, the resistance R is the voltage across it divided by the current flowing through it: R = V / I. As we require 10mA flowing through it, with a voltage of 10V across it, the resistance required is 10V divided by 0.01A, which is 1,000 ohms or 1K.

In summary, R = (VS-VLED) / ILED.

Now, to turn the LED on and off: the GPIO pins are actually mapped as devices in the Linux file system, so using shell commands is easy, although there are many libraries available out there that allow you to control the GPIO using Python, for example. However, so that you don't have to learn a new language, we're going to do everything using shell commands.

The **D0** pin that we are connected to is actually GPIO17 as far as the Raspberry Pi is concerned (take a look at the previous diagram for reference). The first thing we need to do is create file access to this GPIO pin. We do this with the following command:

```
$ sudo echo 17 > /sys/class/gpio/export
```

We then have to set the pin's direction to out:

```
$ sudo echo out > /sys/class/gpio/gpio17/direction
```

Next we can switch the pin on to turn the LED on:

```
$ sudo echo 1 > /sys/class/gpio/gpio17/value
```

To switch the LED off, we use this command:

```
$ sudo echo 0 > /sys/class/gpio/gpio17/value
```

Once we've finished with a GPIO port we can remove its file access:

```
$ sudo echo 17 > /sys/class/gpio/unexport
```

Getting flashy...

We can put these commands together in a single Bash script to create a flashing LED. To create the flashy script, create a new text file in **nano** or some other text editor. Or, as I usually do (don't forget that I'm quite lazy), create the text file on your laptop, and then copy it to the remote Pi using **WinSCP** (although, read my note in the box that follows if you want to prevent some heartache).

The following is the code listing for led-flash.sh:

```bash
#!/bin/bash
sudo echo 17 > /sys/class/gpio/export
sudo echo out > /sys/class/gpio/gpio17/direction
# loop forever
while true
do
  sudo echo 1 > /sys/class/gpio/gpio17/value
  sleep 0.5
  sudo echo 0 > /sys/class/gpio/gpio17/value
  sleep 0.5
done
```

 If you use Windows to create your files, remember to save your files with the end-of-line format being Linux (a single 0x0a or Line Feed character) rather than Windows (0x0a + 0x0d or Line Feed + Carriage Return characters), otherwise you might find that your Bash script does not run properly on the Raspberry Pi. Text editors on Windows, such as the excellent Notepad++, will convert your script line ends for you.

Run the script by calling led-flash.sh (assuming that's what you've called it). If you're in the same directory as the script, this can be done by typing the following:

```
$ sudo bash ./led-flash.sh
```

Since this is an endless loop with the LED flashing on and off at half second intervals, you'll need to break out of it by using *CTRL + C* to stop the script.

Don't forget to remove the GPIO pin from file access by using the following command:

```
$ sudo echo 17 > /sys/class/gpio/unexport
```

Otherwise, you'll see the error, echo: write error: Device or resource busy, if you re-run the script, as the first line tries to set GPIO17 for file access again.

Adding a switch

In this project, we'll see how to connect a switch to a GPIO input and write a shell script to read the state of the switch—that is, whether it's switched on or off.

Connect a switch to your Pi's GPIO27 pin, as shown in the following diagram:

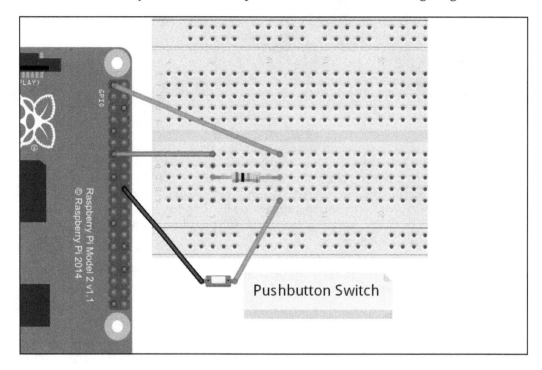

Pushbutton Switch

Pulling yourself together

A really important thing to realize about GPIO inputs is that they are in what's called a *floating state*. This means that, as far as the operating system is concerned, it doesn't know what its reference state is unless it is presented with a known voltage.

This is where our resistor comes into play—it pulls up the GPIO pin to a known voltage of 3.3V, which gives it a default state of HIGH (or binary 1).

When the pushbutton switch is pressed, this takes the GPIO pin to 0V, which is a LOW state (or binary 0).

Here's the circuit diagram for our GPIO switch:

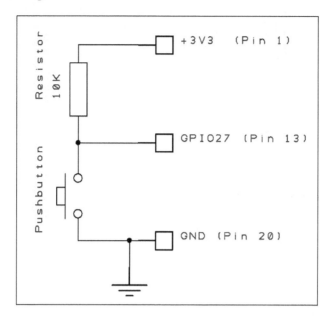

The detection script

Now that we've connected the switch to our Raspberry Pi, we need to write a little script that will detect when the switch has been pushed.

It's similar to the previous LED script shown, but this time we'll set the GPIO pin as an input and read its logic level.

In this project, we've connected our switch to **D2**, which is **GPIO27** (again, refer to the earlier GPIO pin-out diagram). As before, we need to create file access for the pin by entering the following command:

```
$ sudo echo 27 > /sys/class/gpio/export
```

And now, set its direction to `in`:

```
$ sudo echo in > /sys/class/gpio/gpio27/direction
```

We're now ready to read its value, and we can do this with the following command:

```
$ sudo cat /sys/class/gpio/gpio17/value
```

You'll notice that it will have returned 1, or a high state. This is because of the pull-up resistor we were talking about earlier. This means that its default state, when the switch isn't pushed, is high.

When the switch is pushed, the value should be read as 0 or low. If you have more than two hands, you can try this by pushing the button and re-running the command. Or, we can just create a script to poll the switch state.

The code listing for `poll-switch.sh` is as follows:

```bash
#!/bin/bash
sudo echo 27 > /sys/class/gpio/export
sudo echo in > /sys/class/gpio/gpio27/direction

# loop forever
while true
do
  # read the switch state
  SWITCH=$(sudo cat /sys/class/gpio/gpio27/value)

  if [ $SWITCH == 1 ]; then
    #switch not pushed so wait for a second
    sleep 1
  else
    #switch was pushed
    echo "You've pushed my button"
  fi
done
```

When you run the script and then push the button, you should see You've pushed my button scrolling up the console screen until you stop pressing it.

Don't forget that, once we've finished with the GPIO port, we can remove its file access:

```
$ sudo echo 27 > /sys/class/gpio/unexport
```

We've now seen how to easily read a switch input, and the same circuit and script can be used to read other sensors, such as door contact switches, reed switches, or anything else that has an on and off state.

The most elaborate light switch in the world

By combining the two little projects earlier, we can now create a system that will do something useful when the pushbutton switch is pushed — for example, switching on the LED that we also have connected. Granted, we could just connect the LED directly to the switch and a battery, but not only would that be boring, it would defeat the point of what we're trying to do, which is programmatically sensing and controlling things.

Here's the breadboard layout for our elaborate light switch:

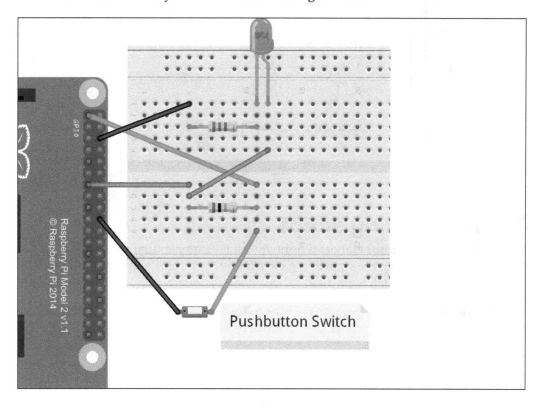

Pushbutton Switch

And here's the circuit diagram:

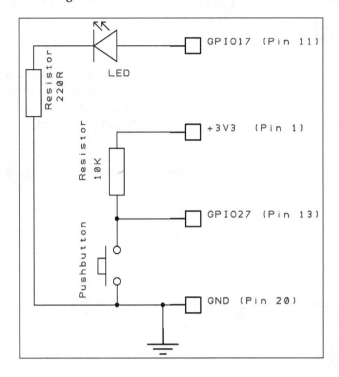

The illuminating script

Our full Bash script for our elaborate light switch is demonstrated next. This will loop endlessly, detecting the state of the switch GPIO pin, and will turn on the LED GPIO pin when the switch is pushed.

The code listing for light-switch.sh is as follows:

```
#!/bin/bash

#set up the LED GPIO pin
sudo echo 17 > /sys/class/gpio/export
sudo echo out > /sys/class/gpio/gpio17/direction

#set up the switch GPIO pin
sudo echo 27 > /sys/class/gpio/export
sudo echo in > /sys/class/gpio/gpio27/direction

# loop forever
while true
```

```
do
  # read the switch state
  SWITCH=$(sudo cat /sys/class/gpio/gpio27/value)

  #0=Pushed 1=Not Pushed
  if [ $SWITCH = "1" ]
  then
    #switch not pushed so turn off LED pin
    sudo echo 0 > /sys/class/gpio/gpio17/value
  else
    #switch was pushed so turn on LED pin
    sudo echo 1 > /sys/class/gpio/gpio17/value
  fi
  #short delay
  sleep 0.5
done
```

So, here we are — we have a script that will detect an input state and do something in response; in this case, it will switch on an LED. We're now forming the basis of how we are going to put together our home security system.

 Remember, don't connect anything to your Raspberry Pi in place of the LED, such as a buzzer or any other device that consumes lots of current. This is likely to irreversibly render your board dead. We'll look at ways, later on in this book, to control devices with higher power requirements.

Summary

In this chapter, we introduced various ways to connect your Raspberry Pi to the outside world by looking at the various interfaces available on the GPIO. We've understood how to connect things to the digital pins on your Raspberry Pi's GPIO connector, and control and read them using simple Bash scripts. In particular, we've safely and properly connected a switch to a digital input pin, which will form the foundation for our home security detection circuits.

In the next chapter, we'll look at ways to expand the number of things we can connect to our Raspberry Pi, overcoming the limitation of having just the 8 digital pins available to us on the GPIO by tapping into other interfaces on the GPIO and building our own input/output expansion board.

3

Extending Your Pi to Connect More Things

We're now going to look at ways to expand the number of things we can connect to our Raspberry Pi, overcoming the limitation of having just the 8 digital pins available. We're going to do this by building our own expansion board to give us what could in theory be an unlimited number of digital inputs and outputs.

We're also going to overcome the limitations of the +3.3V power available to us by building our own +3.3V power supply that taps off the Raspberry Pi's +5V supply.

In this chapter, we will cover the following:

- Looking at the I²C bus in detail
- Learning about serial-to-parallel and parallel-to-serial conversions
- Building a +3.3V power supply
- Building an I2C-based port expander to give us more inputs and outputs
- Looking at alternative ready-made expansion boards

Prerequisites

Along with your Raspberry Pi, you'll need the following parts for the projects in this chapter:

- A copper strip board (or Veroboard®)
- An LD1117V33 voltage regulator
- A 2 x 100nF, 16V ceramic capacitor
- A 10uF, 16V electrolytic capacitor

- A 1 x MCP23017 16-bit port expander IC
- A 4 x 10K-ohm resistor
- A hook-up wire

The I2C bus

In the previous chapter, we briefly touched on the I2C bus (or Inter-Integrated Circuit bus), which is a way to connect multiple devices together using just two wires. I2C was invented in the early 1980s by Philips as a way to link computer peripherals together using a common protocol. You can think of I2C as a kind of early form of USB.

I2C typically operates at relatively low speeds of up to 100kbit/s, compared to much faster interfaces such as Ethernet, which typically operates at up to 1Gbit/s, or USB, which can operate at up to 480Mbit/s. However, this is fast enough to connect basic sensors, display devices, or other peripherals such as real-time clocks — in fact; there are faster versions of the protocol that some devices will support.

Just 2 wires

I2C is a bi-directional serial communication protocol that operates over two wires:

- The **Serial Data Line (SDA)** wire transmits the data to and from the master device. Referring back to the GPIO reference in Chapter 2, *Connecting Things to Your Pi with GPIO*, this is pin 3 of the GPIO connector.
- The **Serial Clock Line (SCL)** wire handles all timing and flow control for the data on the bus. This is pin 5 of the GPIO connector.

You'll remember that we spoke about pull-up resistors, in the previous chapter, which ensure that the GPIO digital inputs are pulled to a known state. Well, this is required for the two lines on the I2C bus, and by default the lines should be pulled high with resistors. However, on the Raspberry Pi, this has already been done for us, so we don't need to worry about it in our case.

What's your address?

So, if we can use just two wires to communicate with multiple devices, how does our Raspberry Pi know which device to talk to? This is where the I2C protocol comes into its own. Each device connected to the bus has its own unique ID, or address, made up of 7-bits or 10-bits. Some devices will allow you to set the address to ensure that it's unique within your system, but other devices have their addresses hardcoded by the manufacturer.

The two addressing methods (7- and 10-bit) are interoperable and you can have devices on the same bus that use either method, since the Raspberry Pi itself supports both methods. So, with a 10-bit addressing scheme, you can see that we can connect a lot of things to our Raspberry Pi using the I2C bus, as compared to the limited number of digital pins on the GPIO!

There is a parallel universe

Data is normally transmitted in serial mode or parallel mode, depending on things such as the required data speed, cable distance, and functionality. Most data communication *between* systems is transmitted in serial mode over a couple of wires, such as the I2C bus mentioned earlier, but this also includes things such as the Ethernet, RS232/422, and USB.

Within a computer system, data is transmitted in parallel mode using *buses* whose width matches the word size of the digital system communicating between chips. In parallel mode, all bits of the data word are transmitted simultaneously over their respective data lines within the bus, rather than as sequential bits along a single line.

The digital I/O pins we've been talking about (including the ones on the Raspberry Pi's GPIO connector) are usually grouped together as a parallel bus. On our system, we'll be using parallel buses (groups of digital I/O pins) that are 8-bits wide. That is, the bus has 8 wires that can be set or read using 8-bit binary values (our word size).

```
Bit 0 (1)      ←--------------------------------------------→
Bit 1 (2)      ←--------------------------------------------→
Bit 2 (4)      ←--------------------------------------------→
Bit 3 (8)      ←--------------------------------------------→
Bit 4 (16)     ←--------------------------------------------→
Bit 5 (32)     ←--------------------------------------------→
Bit 6 (64)     ←--------------------------------------------→
Bit 7 (128)    ←--------------------------------------------→
```

A representation of an 8-bit data bus

So, in the preceding diagram we have the 8 digital I/O wires on our bus. If we wanted to make the bits (or wires) 0, 1, and 4 *high* or *on*, with the rest *low* or *off*, then we'd address the bus and set it to the following values:

- In binary, this would be 00010011
- In hex, this would be *0x13*
- In decimal, this would be 19 (represented by *16+2+1*)

So, in other words, to switch on data lines 0, 1, and 4, we send the byte value, 19, to the bus's address.

Serial-to-parallel conversion

So, now that we know what numbers to send to our bus to switch on or switch off certain digital outputs, or read certain digital inputs, how do we do this using our I2C bus, which is a serial interface?

Fortunately, there are many **integrated circuits** (**ICs**) available that allow us to do this simply and easily. These ICs are called **shift registers** and perform **serial-to-parallel conversions**, taking the data from the serial I2C bus and converting the incoming bits to a parallel representation by setting each of the parallel bus outputs.

When reading the parallel bus data lines as inputs, the reverse happens, converting the bits into a serial form on the I2C bus; this is known as **parallel-to-serial** conversion.

This is quite a simplistic overview and there are many resources available that explain these operations; we'll see this in action later in the chapter, but first…

Give me power

You'll remember from the previous chapter that most things to do with the GPIO operate on a +3.3V level, rather than the +5V level that is often associated with digital circuits. This is the same with our I2C-based shift registers—they need to operate on +3.3V levels as well, in order to work with the Raspberry Pi.

You'll also recall, however, that there's not much +3.3V juice available directly from the Raspberry Pi—in fact, just 50mA. This is really not enough for our interface. So, before we go any further, we're going to build our own +3.3V power supply, which is sufficient for our system.

For our power supply, we're going to use a basic 3.3V **voltage regulator** (type **LD1117V33**) that will take our slightly more plentiful +5V supply from the Raspberry Pi and regulate it to a nice smooth +3.3V supply. We should be able to draw a few hundred milliamps from this supply — enough for the I/O circuitry on our security system.

The parts required for our power supply are as follows:

- A LD1117V33 voltage regulator
- A 100nF, 16V ceramic capacitor
- A 10uF, 16V electrolytic capacitor

Here's the circuit diagram for our +3.3V power supply:

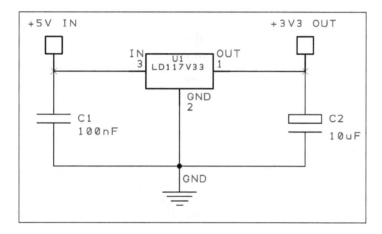

As with all our components, the LD1117V33 regulator is widely available from many electronic component suppliers.

Our power supply can be easily built on a small piece of strip board like this:

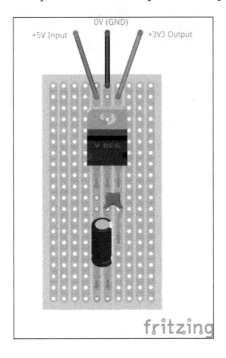

 The strip board is shown from the top in the preceding layout. That is, the copper tracks are on the underside of the board and the components are inserted from the plain top-side and soldered to the strips underneath. In this layout, it's not necessary to cut any of the tracks on the strip board.

Building an I2C expander

Right, now that we've worked out what we need to do to give us more digital I/O pins, and built our power supply for it, we can build our expansion port.

To do this, we're going to use a chip designed exactly for the job: the **MCP23017**, manufactured by Microchip and widely available from electronic suppliers.

The MCP23017 is an integrated circuit that connects directly to the I2C bus (the SDA and SCL pins we talked about earlier) and gives us 16 bi-directional input and output pins. If required, we can connect up to 8 of these chips to the same bus, giving us up to 128 inputs and outputs (yes, I know that I said "virtually unlimited" previously, but I'll explain later).

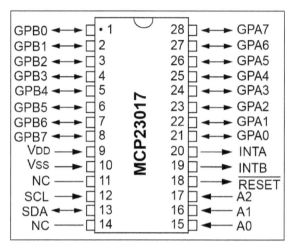

An MCP23017 integrated circuit pinout

 The full datasheet for the MCP23017 is available on Microchip's site, which can be found at www.microchip.com/MCP23017.

The I2C port expander circuit

The basic parts you will need to build your port expander are as follows:

- A 1 x MCP23017 16-bit port expander IC
- A 4 x 10K-ohm resistor
- A 1 x 100nF, 16V ceramic capacitor
- A copper strip board (or Veroboard®)
- A hook-up wire

Here's the circuit diagram for our I2C port expander circuit. It looks complicated, but actually most of the lines are for connections to the outside world:

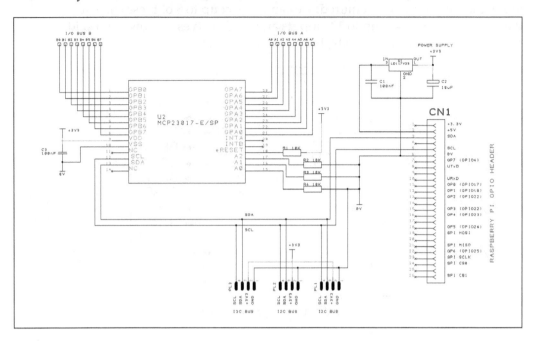

Let's walk through the circuit

On the right-hand side, the connector, CN1, is our Raspberry Pi GPIO connector — note that we're only using four of the pins:

- The +5V Output (Pin 2)
- The I2C SDA (Pin 3)
- The I2C SCL (Pin 5)
- The 0V/GND (Pin 6)

You'll see my friend, the +3.3V regulator (U1, C1, and C2), discussed earlier. This takes the +5V output from the Raspberry Pi and gives us our +3.3V for use by the rest of the circuit.

The main component is U2 — our **MCP23017 port expander** chip. Pins 9 and 10 on the chip are connected to the +3.3V supply and the GND, respectively, and C3 is used as a discoupling capacitor close to the chip to reduce any noise on the power supply.

The MCP23017 can be used as a 16-bit expander, or as 2 x 8-bit expanders. In our circuit, we have split the device to give us 2 x 8-bit busses: I/O Bus A and I/O Bus B. Each pin on the busses can be programmed to work as an input or output.

Connecting things to the input/output pins

The input and output pins on our busses can't usually be connected to things directly – they provide limited current and need to be interfaced correctly to things such as buzzers and lights; they must also be protected against damaging input signals. In the next chapter, we'll learn how to connect safely to our I/O ports.

The I2C SDA/SCL lines from the Raspberry Pi are connected to pins 12 and 13 of the chip. You'll see that there are also additional I2C outputs (PL1 to PL3) to illustrate that we can connect other devices to the I2C bus, such as another MCP23017 chip to give us a further 16 digital I/Os.

Resistor R1 is used to hold the RESET pin (18) high. By bringing this pin low, you can reset the chip.

Resistors R2 to R4 are used to hold the address pins A0 to A2 (pins 15-17) low.

Highs and lows

When we use the terms *high* and *low* in respect to digital pins or inputs, we are simply describing whether the logic level of the pin is at a binary 1 or 0, respectively. Digital pins don't like to be left *floating* – whereby they are neither high nor low – as this can cause unpredictable operations. Therefore, we always make sure they are held at a determined logic level. In general, connecting the pin to 0V (or ground) ensures that it's held at logic level 0, and connecting to the positive supply (e.g. 3.3V) ensures that it's held at logic level 1.

Remember I mentioned earlier that you can connect a large number of devices to the I2C bus in order to give us a virtually unlimited number of I/O pins? Well, actually in many cases, this is not strictly true. This is because of the addressing scheme for I2C devices, which makes all devices identifiable when they are all connected to the same two wires (their unique address). The address of each device is agreed upon in advance by manufacturers to make sure that everyone's devices will work together on the same bus without creating conflicts. As such, the address is pre-programmed into the device.

The MCP23017 has been given its unique base address, but can be modified by changing the address pins A0-A2 high or low; thus, in effect, it can be configured to be one of 8 addresses. This is why you can only have a maximum of 8 of these chips on the same I2C bus, giving us a theoretical maximum of 128 I/O pins (that is, 16 I/Os x 8 chips).

Building your expansion board

This circuit can easily be built on a small piece of stripboard. The following image shows an example of the layout, which looks a bit simpler than the circuit diagram. In the next chapter, we'll learn how to connect up our board and program it so we can check that it works.

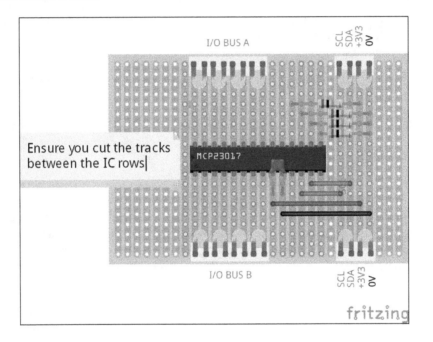

When using stripboard, make sure that you cut the tracks between the two rows of pins on the MCP23017 so that they aren't shorted together. You can buy track cutters, which make this task easy, from many electronic suppliers. Again, on the preceding layout, the copper strips are underneath the board with the components on the plain side.

You might want to add the +3.3V power supply circuit to the same piece of stripboard too, to keep everything contained together.

 In the next chapter, we will learn how to program the device so that we can use it in our home security system.

Using ready-made expansion boards

While it's much more satisfying to build your own stuff, you might want to look at buying some readily available expansion boards for your home security system if you're not yet confident with your soldering iron, or if you just simply don't have the time.

Following are some ready-made expansion boards that you can obtain; they should work as part of our home security system with a bit of modification to our scripts to support the libraries that are required by the hardware.

Hobbytronics MCP23017 expander port kit

This kit is almost identical to our own circuit in the previous section of this chapter. The kit comes with an MCP23017, a PCB, and various connectors. The boards are designed to be daisy-chained together so that you can have multiple expanders to give you more input/output ports. Note that this kit is not pre-built and requires soldering, but I thought I'd include it because it's the board that I use to build such systems when prototyping. You can get it directly from Hobbytronics at `http://bit.ly/mcp23017`.

PiFace Digital I/O expansion board

The **PiFace Digital I/O expansion board** is a pre-built version of our board, but it uses the **MSP23S17** chip variant that operates over the **SPI bus** instead of the I2C bus. The board is designed with 8 inputs and 8 outputs, as well as several additional pieces of hardware including a couple of relays, some LEDs, and some switches. Note that the code in this book for our system will need to be modified to work with this board, since it uses a different interface and different libraries. It's available from Farnell element14 at `http://bit.ly/2434230`.

The PiFace Digital I/O Expansion Board

Gertboard

The **Gertboard** is a Raspberry Pi add-on board designed by Gert van Loo — one of the hardware engineers involved in the original design of the Raspberry Pi.

It's a very capable and reasonably-priced board that comes fully assembled and features 12 buffered input/output lines, open collector drivers for switching on devices that need a fair bit of current (such as sounders and lights), plus a digital-to-analog converter.

You can only connect one of these boards to your Raspberry Pi, so if you need more I/O lines you'll need to use something else as well. But it's a great board to experiment with. Interestingly, it features an **ATmega microcontroller**, which is the same as the one that the Arduino uses, and you can, in fact, use the **Arduino** development environment for the device.

Once again, the code in this book for our system will need to be modified to work with this board.

The Gertboard is available from Farnell element14 at `http://bit.ly/2250034`.

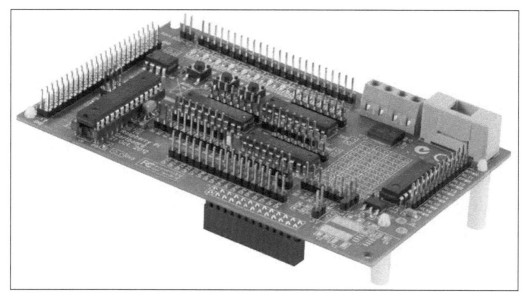

Assembled Gertboard

Summary

We've now looked at the I2C bus in detail, and learned how to build an expansion port using this interface so that we can connect many more things to our Raspberry Pi, rather than being restricted to just the 8 digital I/O pins offered by the Raspberry Pi's GPIO port. In addition to that, we explored other ready-made boards that can be used to connect lots of things to our Raspberry Pi. We have also built a power supply that will give us more +3.3V power than we can obtain from the Raspberry Pi directly.

In the next chapter, we'll start to actually connect things to our home security system, such as magnetic sensors and other types of contact devices, and learn how to program our I2C expansion port using Bash scripts so that we can read the state of our sensors and switch on warning LEDs. We'll also start developing the control scripts for our system, which will allow us to arm and disarm the system and add delay timers.

4

Adding a Magnetic Contact Sensor

Now that we have built our port expander hardware, we need to learn how to program it so that our Raspberry Pi can detect the things that we connect to it as part of our home security system. We will begin by connecting switches to our system in the form of magnetic sensors—the most common component used in home security systems to detect intrusions through doors and windows.

In this chapter we will cover the following topics:

- Learning about reed switches and how they work as door sensors
- Enabling and setting up the I2C bus on the Raspberry Pi
- Connecting our sensor to an input on our port expander
- Learning how to access our I2C port expander from a Bash script
- Writing a script that will detect the state of our door sensor
- Looking at other types of contact sensors that can be connected and programmed in the same way

Prerequisites

You'll need the following parts for the exercises in this chapter:

- Our Raspberry Pi and Port Expander board
- 8 x 10K ohm resistors
- A magnetic door sensor and magnet
- A hook-up wire
- A 4-core alarm wire

The working of magnetic contact sensors

A **reed switch** is essentially what makes up our **magnetic contact sensor**. A reed switch comprises two metal contacts made of magnetic material (called reeds) placed inside a glass envelope. When the contacts touch, the switch is on, and when they spring apart, the switch is off and the circuit is broken. The way to control these contacts is by means of a **magnetic field** that makes or breaks the circuit when it is near to the switch.

A normally open (NO) type of reed switch is normally switched off until a magnet comes close to the switch, which then pulls the contacts together.

A normally closed (NC) variety works the other way with the switch being normally on until the magnet comes close to the switch, pulling the two contacts apart.

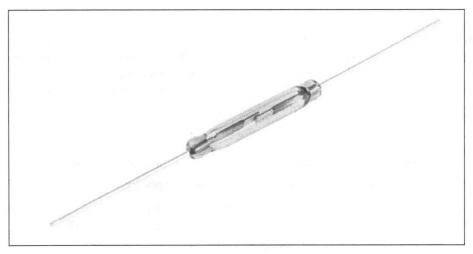

A typical type of reed switch

You can now see how a magnetic reed switch can be a useful sensor in security applications, and in particular for our home security system, to detect when **doors** and **windows** are opened and closed. We simply put a reed switch on the door frame and connect it to our security system, with the magnet placed opposite the switch on the actual door. When the door opens and closes, it makes or breaks the contacts in our reed switch.

Reed switches and their magnets, which are designed for security systems, usually come enclosed in little plastic housings, making them easy to screw onto the door and frame.

A door-frame-mounted magnetic sensor containing a reed switch (Type: Cherry MP201801)

The magnetic sensor is mounted on the door frame (obviously, so it can connect to the alarm circuit wires), while the respective magnet will be attached to the door, close enough to the edge such that the sensor contacts connect (or break, depending on the type) when the magnet is directly opposite it.

A respective door-mounted magnetic actuator (Type: Cherry AS201801)

Setting up the I2C port expander

Now that we have built our port expander, we need to get it ready to connect our sensors to. First, we need to install the tools on the Raspberry Pi to allow us to use the I2C bus and program devices connected to it, including the MCP23017 chip that makes up our port expander.

 Don't connect your port expander to the Raspberry Pi until after you've set up the I2C bus on your system.

Enabling the I2C Bus

It's highly likely that the module for using the I2C bus hasn't been loaded by default. Fortunately, doing this is fairly straightforward and can be done using the Raspberry Pi configuration tool. Perform the following steps:

1. Launch the Raspberry Pi configuration tool with the following command:

   ```
   $ sudo raspi-config
   ```

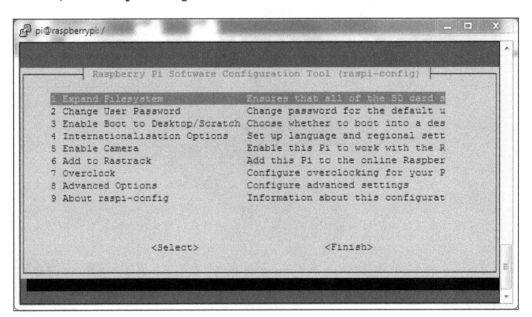

2. Select option 8: `Advanced Options`.

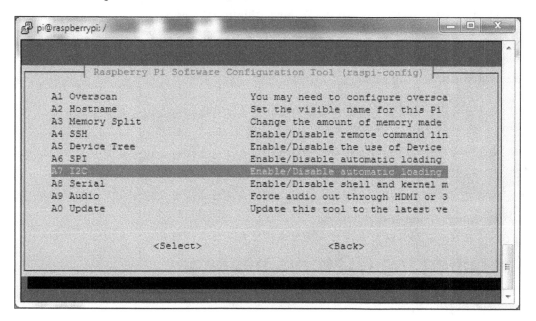

3. Select Option A7: `I2C`.

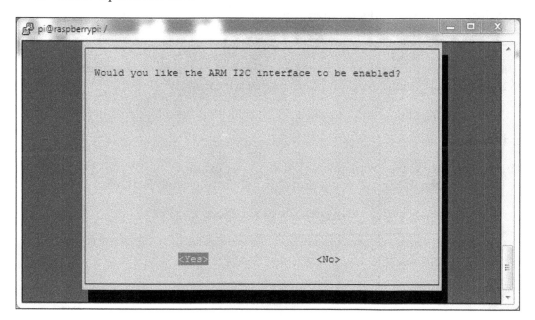

4. Select <Yes>.

5. Reboot your Raspberry Pi for the setting to take effect.

Now that the I2C bus has been enabled, we need to set up the operating system so that the required modules are loaded each time the system boots. To do this, perform the following steps:

1. Edit the **Modules file** using the following line:

   ```
   $ sudo nano /etc/modules
   ```

2. Add the following lines to the file:

   ```
   i2c-bcm2708

   i2c-dev
   ```

3. Save the file and exit Nano.

Installing the I2C tools package

So that we can easily access the I2C bus using Bash scripts, we need to install the `i2c-tools` package:

```
$ sudo apt-get install i2c-tools
```

Once installed, we should shutdown our system:

```
sudo shutdown -h now
```

After activity has stopped, switch off your Raspberry Pi, connect your port expander to the GPIO port, and power it back up so that we can start using it.

As a quick sanity check, you can see if I2C support has been loaded by typing:

```
$ ls /dev/i2c-*
```

This should give you a list of at least one bus — for example, `/dev/i2c-1` — if the module is loaded. If it's not, you'll probably get the following response:

ls: cannot access /dev/i2c-*: No such file or directory

In this case, you'll need to check back through the previous steps as something hasn't happened properly.

Finding our devices

The i2c-tools package installs several different tools to help us use our port expander attached to the bus. The i2cdetect tool allows us to find I2C buses and devices attached to the busses.

To get a list of I2C busses on our system, type the following:

```
$ sudo i2cdetect -l
```

You should get the following response:

pi@raspberrypi ~ $ sudo i2cdetect -l

i2c-1 i2c   20804000.i2c   I2C adapter

The preceding output shows that we have one I2C bus, and this will be the one connected to our GPIO. *Note that earlier models of the Raspberry Pi may return the device ID as being i2c-0.*

We can now use the tool to scan for all of the devices attached to our bus. We do this by specifying the bus ID, as in the following command:

```
$ sudo i2cdetect 1
```

With nothing attached to the I2C bus (that is, without our port expander attached) we'd expect to see the following output:

```
pi@raspberrypi ~ $ sudo i2cdetect 1
WARNING! This program can confuse your I2C bus, cause data loss and
worse!
I will probe file /dev/i2c-1.
I will probe address range 0x03-0x77.
Continue? [Y/n] Y
     0  1  2  3  4  5  6  7  8  9  a  b  c  d  e  f
00:          -- -- -- -- -- -- -- -- -- -- -- -- --
10: -- -- -- -- -- -- -- -- -- -- -- -- -- -- -- --
20: -- -- -- -- -- -- -- -- -- -- -- -- -- -- -- --
30: -- -- -- -- -- -- -- -- -- -- -- -- -- -- -- --
40: -- -- -- -- -- -- -- -- -- -- -- -- -- -- -- --
50: -- -- -- -- -- -- -- -- -- -- -- -- -- -- -- --
60: -- -- -- -- -- -- -- -- -- -- -- -- -- -- -- --
70: -- -- -- -- -- -- -- --
pi@raspberrypi ~ $
```

Nothing found on the I2C bus

With our port expander attached, we should see the following output:

```
pi@raspberrypi ~ $ i2cdetect 1
WARNING! This program can confuse your I2C bus, cause data loss and
worse!
I will probe file /dev/i2c-1.
I will probe address range 0x03-0x77.
Continue? [Y/n] Y
     0  1  2  3  4  5  6  7  8  9  a  b  c  d  e  f
00:          -- -- -- -- -- -- -- -- -- -- -- -- --
10: -- -- -- -- -- -- -- -- -- -- -- -- -- -- -- --
20: 20 -- -- -- -- -- -- -- -- -- -- -- -- -- -- --
30: -- -- -- -- -- -- -- -- -- -- -- -- -- -- -- --
40: -- -- -- -- -- -- -- -- -- -- -- -- -- -- -- --
50: -- -- -- -- -- -- -- -- -- -- -- -- -- -- -- --
60: -- -- -- -- -- -- -- -- -- -- -- -- -- -- -- --
70: -- -- -- -- -- -- -- --
pi@raspberrypi ~ $
```

Our I2C port expander slave device can be found at the address, 0x20 (32 decimal).

 The preceding address is the location of our MCP23017 chip connected to the I2C bus. If you don't see this, then there's probably a wiring issue and you'll need to go back and check.

You'll recall that we can add up to 8 of these devices to the I2C bus by setting the A0-A2 pins to a unique address. If A0 is set to high, then the address of the device will be shown as 0x21 (33 decimal) — and up to 0x27 (39 decimal), if all pins are high.

Setting up the port expander

As discussed in the previous chapter, we can have 2 x 8-bit busses on our port expander, with each pin being defined as an input or output. On the expander board we built, we called them I/O BUS A and I/O BUS B.

To configure the MCP23017 chip on the I2C bus, we can send it the appropriate commands using the **i2cset** tool we installed earlier.

On our home security system, we are going to assign all of the pins on BUS A as inputs for connecting our sensors to it. To do this, we use the following command:

```
$ sudo i2cset -y 1 0x20 0x00 0xFF
```

 What does this command mean?
- -y: This runs the command without user interaction.
- 1: This is the ID of the bus (for example, `i2c-1`).
- 0x20: This is the address of the chip.
- 0x00: This is the data register on the chip (in this case, the PORT A pin assignment).
- 0xFF: This is the Value loaded into the data register (in this case, all pins as inputs—binary %11111111).

You can check that the data register has been set correctly by reading it using the following:

```
$ sudo i2cget -y 1 0x20 0x00
```

This should return a value of `0xFF`, which is the value we set earlier.

Connecting our magnetic contact sensor

Now that we've got our port expander working with the Raspberry Pi, we can start connecting things to it and create the scripts that will monitor the sensors on the input pins.

Let's go back to our port expander stripboard that was built in the previous chapter and connect our magnetic sensor. But first, we need to ensure that all of our inputs are pulled low by default using 10Kohm resistors. This prevents them from being in a *floating* state and giving us spurious data when we read the port's data.

In the following diagram, I've connected the pull-down resistors externally, but you may want to include them directly on the stripboard. Toward the end of this book, we'll have a new board layout that brings everything that we've been prototyping so far together in a single solution.

To check the port's input value, we use the `i2cget` command:

```
$ sudo i2cget -y 1 0x20 0x12
```

This should return `0x00`, which means all inputs are off (binary %00000000).

What does this command mean?

- -y: This runs the command without user interaction.
- 1: This is the ID of the bus (for example i2c-1).
- 0x20: This is the address of the chip.
- 0x12: This is the data register on the chip (in this case, the PORT A read value).

Now let's connect one side of our magnetic sensor's reed switch to data pin 0 of BUS A (which we'll call GPA0 for reference), and the other side to our +3.3V line. By default, the switch is normally open (NO), which means that the input is still pulled low by the resistor.

But when you move the accompanying magnet near to the sensor switch (for example, if the door is closed), the switch will close, pulling the input high to the +3.3V line. If you read the port's input value now, by running the same command, you should see that it returns 0x01, indicating that the first bit is high (binary %00000001).

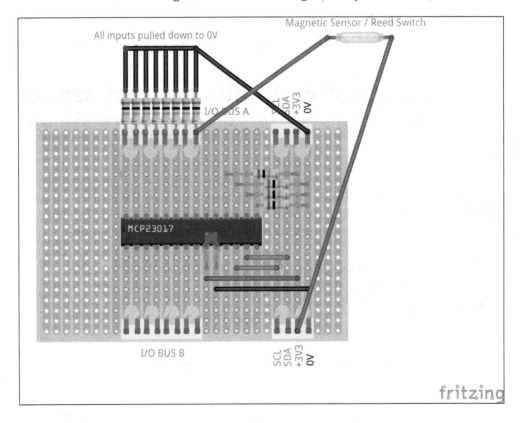

Monitoring the sensor

Now that we have everything in place and our magnetic sensor is detecting whether the door is closed, we can monitor this sensor with a simple Bash script that uses the I2C tool commands that we installed earlier.

The code listing for `poll-magnetic-switch.sh` is as follows:

```bash
#!/bin/bash
sudo i2cset -y 1 0x20 0x00 0xFF

# loop forever
while true
do
  # read the sensor state
  SWITCH=$(sudo i2cget -y 1 0x20 0x12)

  if [ $SWITCH == "0x01" ]
  then
    #contact closed so wait for a second
    echo "The door is closed!"
    sleep 1
  else
    #contact was opened
    echo "The door is open!"
  fi
done
```

When you run the script and then push the button, you should see "**The door is open!**" scrolling up the console screen until you stop pressing it.

By combining this with our elaborate light switch project in chapter 2, we can switch on the LED connected to GPIO17 when the door is opened:

```bash
#!/bin/bash

#set up the LED GPIO pin
sudo echo 17 > /sys/class/gpio/export
sudo echo out > /sys/class/gpio/gpio17/direction

#set up port expander
sudo i2cset -y 1 0x20 0x00 0xFF
```

```
# loop forever
while true
do
  # read the sensor state
  SWITCH=$(sudo i2cget -y 1 0x20 0x12)

  if [ $SWITCH == "0x01" ]
  then
    #switch not pushed so turn off LED pin
    sudo echo 0 > /sys/class/gpio/gpio17/value
  else
    #switch was pushed so turn on LED pin
    sudo echo 1 > /sys/class/gpio/gpio17/value
  fi
  #short delay
  sleep 0.5
done
```

 Later, as we add more sensors to different input pins, we will need to be able to detect which one has been triggered. We'll look at writing a Bash function later in the book, which will parse the returned hex value from the i2cget command, and tell us exactly which of the 8 inputs is high.

Anti-tamper circuits

If you take a closer look at our system, you might realize that depending on whether you are detecting normally open or normally closed sensor switches, it is possible to tamper with the sensor channel by simply cutting the wire. So, in the case of a normally open switch, it wouldn't activate the monitoring system if the wires were cut, as it would always appear to be open, even if the switch was closed.

To mitigate this, most alarm systems feature a 4-core wiring system to connect the sensor devices to the main control board—two cores are used to connect the sensor and two are used to create an **anti-tamper loop**, which then itself forms a sensor input for monitoring.

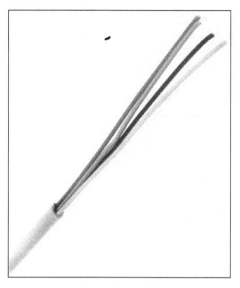

4-core alarm cable

Take a look at the following circuit so that you see what I mean:

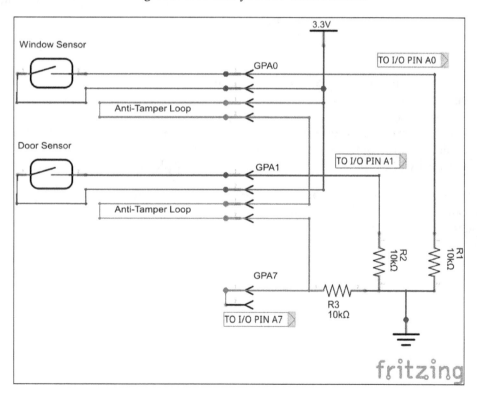

In this circuit, we have two sensors: one for monitoring a window and one for monitoring a door. These are connected to the I/O BUS A inputs, 0 and 1 (or GPA0 and GPA1, as we like to call them). As before, they are pulled down to 0V by resistors but, when switches are closed, the positive voltage rail takes the inputs high.

However, we've also added an anti-tamper loop throughout the whole system, which is connected to GPA7 for monitoring. The loop is daisy-chained through each of the cables connecting the sensors to the controller board. All the time the loop is intact, the input GPA7 is kept high, but if the cable is cut anywhere, the current will stop flowing through it and the resistor, R3, will pull the input low. This will then be detected by the monitoring script.

Many security sensor products provide a facility to terminate anti-tamper loop wires within them.

So, in our home security system, we're going to assign GPA7 as our anti-tamper loop.

Getting into the zone

It may have occurred to you by now that even a modest-sized property could require plenty of door and window sensors; thus, if we used one input for each sensor, we'd soon run out unless we put more and more port expanders onto the system. The same is true for commercially available security systems.

So, the way this is dealt with is by creating **zones**, with each zone containing a group of sensors. A bedroom, for example, may be defined as one zone with a window sensor, a door sensor, and movement detector forming that zone. In this scenario, each sensor is connected to the next in a series (or daisy-chained); if one of them triggers, it will alert the monitoring system that there was a trigger in the zone. Obviously, though, it may not necessarily be the actual detector, which in most applications isn't really an issue.

However, this can introduce some challenges when we're considering mixing normally open and normally closed type sensors within a zone, but this is something we will explore later on in this book.

The other sensors you can use are listed as follows:

- **Hall Effect Sensor**: Hall-effect sensors are simple electronic chips that are used to detect magnetic fields placed near them. They are not dissimilar to the reed switch we've been using; however, because they are electronic devices, they are able to measure the degree of proximity in relation to the magnet (or the strength of magnetism), rather than being just on or off, as is the case with the reed switch. Also, because they are solid-state, they could be seen as being more reliable than mechanical switches.

A low-cost hall effect sensor – Allegro Microsystems A1302KUA-T

- Pressure Mat Sensors: Pressure mats are used to detect a person standing or walking on them, and can be placed under a floor mat to hide them from sight. They can even be used in a chair to detect people sitting on it. Essentially, they are switches, just like the reed switch, except that they are activated by the pressure of walking on them, and so, can be wired and used in exactly the same way as for our magnetic sensor circuits.

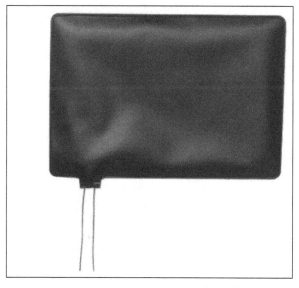

A pressure switch can be used under a front-door mat

Summary

In this chapter, we got our I2C-based port expander configured and working, and we experimented with it by connecting a magnetic sensor—one of the most commonly used sensors in security systems. We've also learned how to interact with I2C devices using Bash scripts, and how to read and write data to and from these devices.

In addition, we should now be beginning to understand the various elements and building blocks of a security system, including anti-tamper loops and zones. These are concepts that will prepare us for later on in the book, when we start to piece all of this together and build our final, all-encompassing system.

In the next chapter, we will look at passive infra-red motion detectors, how they work, and how we can connect the wired and wireless types to our home security system. We'll also learn how to create log files based on events using Bash scripts so that we can maintain a history of detector states as they change.

5
Adding a Passive Infrared Motion Sensor

In the previous chapter, we started adding basic but commonly used magnetic switch sensors to our home security system and reading their status to protect doors and windows from intrusion. We also looked at how we can divide our home into zones, such as by individual rooms, so that we can group our sensors into logical circuits, which can then be identified as part of these zones rather than as individual sensor inputs.

We will now add **motion sensors** to our system in the form of **Passive Infra-Red (PIR)** detectors. These detectors come in a variety of types, and you may have seen them lurking in the corners of rooms. Fundamentally, they all work in the same way, which is detecting the presence of body heat within a certain range; so, they are commonly used to trigger alarm systems when somebody (or something, such as a pet cat) enters a room.

A typical PIR motion sensor (type GardScan QX-PIR)

In this chapter, we will:

- Learn how PIR detectors work and how they are set up
- Connect a wired PIR detector to an input on our port expander
- Start using a 12V power supply instead of 3.3V in our zone circuits
- Learn how to interface 12V circuits safely with our GPIO ports
- Learn how to connect a 433 MHz wireless receiver to our Raspberry Pi
- Connect a remote-controlled switch to our system using 433 MHz radio signals
- Write a script that will detect and log the state of our detector inputs when it changes

Prerequisites

You'll need the following parts for this chapter (apart from the components used in the previous chapter):

- A passive infrared detector, the wired type (this is available from any DIY store)
- A 4N25/4N35 opto-isolator
- A 1N4148 diode
- A 1-Kohm resistor
- A 10-Kohm resistor
- A 433 MHz receiver module and remote transmitter (this is optional)
- A 12V power supply
- A hook-up wire
- A 6 core alarm wire

Passive infrared sensors explained

You might not realize it, but all objects radiate heat energy (including your coffee table); it's just that you can't see it because heat consists essentially of infrared waves, which are invisible to the human eye (exactly the same as your TV remote control). These waves can, however, be detected by electronic devices designed for such a purpose, such as the infrared receiver in your TV that detects the energy emitted by your remote control when the buttons are pressed.

You probably do realize, however, that living things such as us, our cat, and the mouse under the floorboards generate quite a bit of heat. Passive infrared motion sensors used in security systems and automatic lights are designed to detect this level of heat. The term *passive* is used because the sensors themselves do not radiate any energy for detection purposes—instead, they just detect the infrared radiation emitted by objects. This is notably different from devices such as ultrasonic sensors and radars, which rely on detecting reflections from objects of the pulses of energy that the sensors send out.

PIR sensors need to be a little smart because they effectively have to cope with constantly varying temperatures in the room. They settle on the background temperature of the room they are in, such as that of a wall or floor that they point to. When an object, such as one of us or our cat, moves between the detector unit and the background object, the temperature in front of the sensor rises to the body temperature quickly, and this in turn triggers the system.

Setting up your PIR sensor

PIR sensor devices come in many formats, including different materials in sensor chips and the lens in front of the sensor view window that can widely affect the range, field of view, and sensitivity of the device. Therefore, your best guide to setting up a sensor will usually be in that little bit of instruction paper that comes with it.

However, regardless of the type of PIR sensor you have, here are some general guidelines when considering where you mount your sensor in order to avoid false triggers:

- Ensure that the device is mounted on a solid foundation and not affected by vibration
- Never mount it in a location where direct or reflected sunlight can be picked up by the lens
- Similarly, never mount the device facing or above heat sources
- Don't mount the unit in draughty locations as this will affect its background temperature calibration

The location of the unit also depends on the area you want to protect. You may want to detect people entering your living room from the hallway, so your coverage area could be defined as being from the corner of the room where the device is mounted to the living room door.

PIR sensors usually offer a fixed field of view (for example 90 or 110 degrees) but have a varying range, depending on the angle at which they are pointing down and the height at which they are located.

In my system, I will use a Gardscan QX PIR Detector for my wired units, which is a pretty good, low-cost unit available from RS Components (the order code is 493-1289). This unit has a field view of 110 degrees and a range of up to 12 meters, depending on the configurable down angle that it's mounted at. The coverage patterns for this particular unit, as taken from its datasheet, are shown in the following figure. Note that from these patterns not every part of the area in front of the device is covered, which is possibly not quite what you expect. This is why positioning the units in accordance with the device's datasheet is so important.

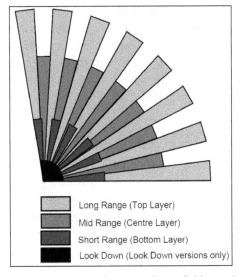

GardScan QX-PIR coverage pattern for its 110 degree field view (top/plan view)

Here is a diagram of the side view as well:

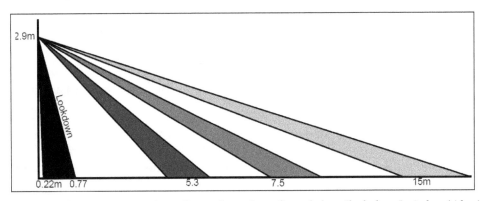

GardScan QX-PIR coverage pattern depending on the angle configured plus a "look-down" window (side view)

Give me power (again)

Before we can go on to connect off-the-shelf security devices to our alarm system, we need to have a power supply that's compatible with such devices. Typically, alarm circuits and their devices use a 12V supply with enough current to drive all the devices and the alarm control system itself.

Fortunately, this is not too difficult to sort out, but it is something we need to do now; otherwise, we won't be able to connect and power our PIR sensors. The easiest way to do this is to buy a high-quality 12V mains adapter that provides a nice regulated supply. These are readily available from online stores or electronics suppliers. Alternatively, you can build your own 12V regulated supply and add it to the power supply strip board that we built in *Chapter 3*, *Extending Your Pi to Connect More Things*.

 Another option is to use battery-powered PIR sensors, which means that you wouldn't have to power the unit from the security system's panel itself; however, it obviously also means that the batteries would need replacing from time to time. The wireless PIR we will look at later in this chapter is battery-powered.

We'll take a look at handling higher-voltage sensor circuits later on in this chapter so that we don't blow up our home security control circuits or the Raspberry Pi.

Connecting our PIR motion sensor

Commercially available alarm systems connect to their devices using a 4 core or 6 core alarm cable. In the previous chapter, we used a 4 core cable because we were connecting a switch that needed two wires plus an antitamper loop, which needed another two wires.

For our PIR sensor circuit, we need the same four wires; however, we also need to send power to the device from the control panel, so an additional two wires are needed for this—hence the requirement for a 6 core cable.

The following diagram shows the wiring connections for my GardScan PIR sensor, but this is in fact typical for most off-the-shelf security system devices:

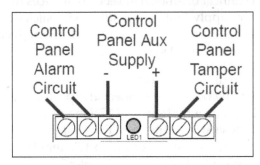

Typical connections for security system sensor devices

Similar to the magnetic contact sensors that we looked at in the previous chapter, devices can come with either a **normally closed (NC)** or a **normally open (NO)** alarm. This particular device has a normally closed output, which means that the alarm circuit will be broken when the detector is triggered. This is the preferred configuration for our sensor devices as this means that they can be wired in a series within each of our zones.

We can now add this sensor device into the alarm circuit that we started putting together in the previous chapter. The following diagram shows the circuit for all our sensors so far wired into a single zone:

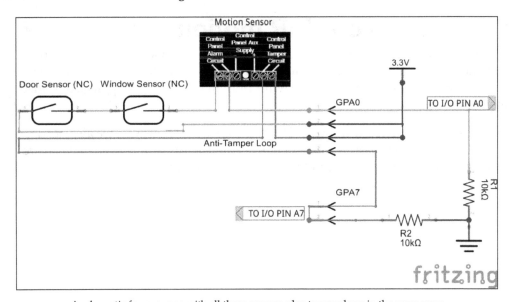

A schematic for our zone with all three sensors plus tamper loop in the same zone

Up until now, we used the +3.3V power supply to pass through the sensor switches and alarm circuit. In fact, this is not a good idea, and we've been doing this only for convenience to test out our GPIO inputs.

In reality, and in our final system, we really should use a 12V supply to pass through the sensor and antitamper circuits. This is because a higher voltage travels better through the system and is less susceptible to noise, which could prevent triggering or cause false triggering. This also makes it compatible with commercially available systems and accessories.

12V alarm zone circuits

Making our zone circuits use 12V instead of 3.3V is as simple as changing the power supply, and in fact all of sensors we used so far can handle 12V power passed through their switches.

However, if we were to present the 12V circuit to the inputs on our GPIO port on the Raspberry Pi or our port expander, we would expect to see some magic smoke and smell something burning. So, we need to add some circuitry that allows us to use 12V alarm circuits as well as protect our control board inputs.

Alarm circuit protection

An effective way to protect our zone inputs from 12V alarm inputs is to use a little low-cost device called an opto-isolator. As the name suggests, this isolates the alarm circuit from the digital inputs of the control board using light.

Inside an opto-isolator (also called an opto-coupler) is an infrared LED, which transmits light to a photo-transistor when a current is passed through it, thus switching it on. The circuits are electrically isolated as they are controlled only by light.

The 4N25 (shown in the preceding image) and 4N35 are low-cost, 6-pin opto-coupler devices, and most manufactures tend to use the pin layout shown in the following diagram:

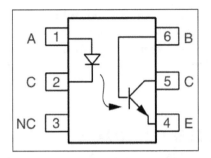

Now that we know how we will couple our 12V alarm circuit with the inputs on our control panel, let's build the entire circuit, which we'll use for each of the zones that we add to our system.

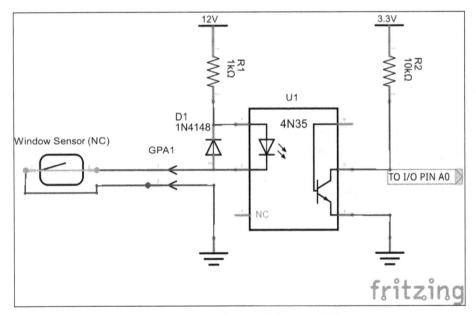

A 12V zone circuit optically isolated from the GPIO input

How it works

At this time, we're assuming that our zone circuits are normally closed — that is, the alarm triggers when the circuit is broken.

The 12V supply is passed through the LED of the opto-isolator with the current being limited by the 1-Kohm resistor. The 1N4148 diode, in reverse, is there to protect the opto-coupler from reverse-polarity voltages.

 The 1-Kohm resistor is calculated from the fact that we have a 12V supply and a forward voltage drop (Vf) of 1.2V across the LED with a current (If) of about 10 mA.

While the alarm circuit is closed, the current flows, and the LED is on. This keeps the transistor on and the input to the GPIO port is held low. If the alarm circuit is broken, the opto-coupler LED switches off, and this in turn switches off the transistor. The GPIO input is then pulled high by the 10-Kohm resistor.

This is quite simple but effective, eh?

The other advantage of this circuit is that it should fail positive – that is, if the opto-coupler should fail for any reason, the alarm input on the GPIO port should be pulled high, thus triggering it rather than it just failing silently.

Wireless PIR motion sensors

Wireless motion sensors are now commonly available at a low cost, allowing them to be installed practically anywhere without any wiring from the alarm control panel. Some of them still require an external power supply, but many operate on batteries. The alarm system must contain a wireless receiver compatible with the wireless sensor.

In this section, we'll take a look at how we can use our Raspberry Pi-based security system with wireless receiver devices.

433-MHz wireless alarm systems

Wireless systems use an unlicensed radio frequency to communicate between the various components of an alarm system. In the UK, the two most popular frequencies used are **433 MHz** and **868 MHz**. While the more recent systems now use the 868-MHz frequency, 433 MHz is still in widespread use as it has a slightly longer range than an 868-MHz system. However, the 433-MHz band is also used by many other devices, which makes it congested, whereas 868 MHz is generally used only for alarm systems.

While wireless security systems can be convenient, it's important to understand the advantages and disadvantages of using wireless rather than wired systems.

The advantages are as follows:

- Their ease and speed of installation
- Their ease of removal, which means that you can take them anywhere with you
- Expanding the system in the future can be easier, with most systems automatically detecting new units

The disadvantages are as follows:

- They are more expensive than wired systems, sometimes three or four times the cost
- They are not as secure as wired systems and cannot achieve a security grading greater than two in accordance with European Standard BSEN 50131 (although, this grade is suitable for domestic properties)
- Wireless devices need to have their batteries replaced at regular intervals
- Wireless systems are less reliable and susceptible to interference and even radio jamming

Connecting a 433-MHz receiver

In the past, it was possible to roll out your own 433-MHz receiver for the Raspberry Pi using an inexpensive receiver, such as the XY-MV-5V module along with the **433-Util** library that was put together by a guy called Mark Wolfe, a contributor on GitHub. Essentially, he gathered together code relating to 433-MHz communications and put it all into this library. Originally developed for Arduino, this has now been ported to the Raspberry Pi.

You can then use a readily available transmitter, such as a key fob or any other 433-MHz transmitter, and take a look at the incoming code as you press each button on the transmitter.

A XY-MK-5V Generic 433-MHz receiver module

Finding a suitable 433-MHz receiver should be easy as websites such as Amazon and eBay are awash with them, and they cost as little as a couple of pounds.

 Note that the 433-MHz band is a free for many types of devices. As such, there are various different types of receiver, and although they may all state that they are 433-MHz receivers, they can operate using AM or FM, and some only detect certain types of data. Some, such as the Quasar QAM range, may also require special decoder chips in order to read transmitted data and may only work with paired transmitters.

The receiver module can pick up signals from a key fob remote control, such as the one shown in the following image (this can be picked up from the home security section of any local DIY store), which gets an output as a series of square waves. These square waves are then decoded by the 433-Util software.

A Novar/Blyss 433MHz wireless remote control

I liked this particular remote control because I thought it would be good as the **arm** and **disarm** device for our home security system. I will talk about arming and disarming in *Chapter 8, A Miscellany of Things*, where we will look at the ways to achieve this.

The alternative approach (because we have no choice)

I started off the previous section with the words "In the past...". This is because in recent times, I've not been able to get the 433-Util software working with receiver modules, which used to work in the past). I'm not entirely sure why this is so; however, I can only guess that because the software uses "bit banging" to decode incoming data signals, the timing is no longer correct, perhaps because later Raspberry Pi boards are faster and therefore mess up the routines.

What is bit banging?

Bit banging is a way of using software for serial communication instead of dedicated hardware. The software is responsible for all the parameters of the signal, including timing, levels, and synchronization. Bit banging can be seen as a bit of a hack, but it does allow the implementation of different protocols at a very low cost without any hardware changes.

So, in order to make our lives easier (and actually make the device work on all flavors of Pi), we will resort to using a dedicated receiver module that you can pick up for less than £5 on Amazon and doesn't require all this software bit banging nonsense. You'll notice from the following image that it still uses a similar XY-MK-5V radio receiver; it's just that the host board decodes the signals for us and switches a relay on or off in response to a command from the remote control.

If you're still interested in the 433-Util software project and want to try and roll out your own receiver, you can find the original project at https://github.com/ninjablocks/433Utils.

A Hielec transmitter fob and receiver module, available on Amazon

The fact that it just switches a relay on and off means that we can easily implement this in our home security system because it simply acts as a switch. When you press the button on the transmitter, the relay switches the contacts on; press it again, and the relay switches off. The screw terminals on the board provide us with access to the relay terminals.

The receiver wiring diagram

As we are just dealing with a switch input, we can use the same circuit as we did with the zone circuit earlier but connected to our arm/disarm GPIO input, which we'll determine in *Chapter 9, Putting It All Together*.

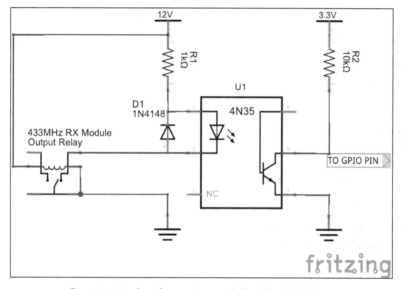

Circuit to interface the receiver module with a GPIO input

When the receiver module switches the relay on, this will complete the 12V circuit through the opto-coupler's LED by turning it on. This will make the transistor pull the GPIO pin down to ground, giving it a low input.

You can use this type of circuit for any paired receiver for the wireless security devices that you want to use in your system.

Logging detection data

With any system, it's useful to be able to log data when something happens. We can do this with our detectors too by writing to a log file every time a detector in a zone is triggered. This way, you can keep a log of every time someone enters a room, which you can review at a later date even if the system isn't armed. You can also keep a log of when the system is armed and disarmed.

Here's a simple script that shows you how to do this whenever an event happens on our zones connected to the GPIO inputs:

```bash
#!/bin/bash

#set up the I2C expansion port
sudo i2cset -y 1 0x20 0x00 0xFF

#reset status
CURR_STATE="0x00"
LAST_STATE="0x00"

#path to the log file
LOG_FILE="/etc/pi-alarm/zones.log"

# loop forever
while true
do
  # read the gpio inputs
  CURR_STATE=$(sudo i2cget -y 1 0x20 0x12)

   #check if state has changed
   if [ "$CURR_STATE" != "$LAST_STATE" ]
  then
    #write change to log file
      TIMESTAMP=`date "+%Y-%m-%d %H:%M:%S"`
     echo "$TIMESTAMP Zone Status Changed from $LAST_STATE to
     $CURR_STATE" > $LOG_FILE
   fi
   $LAST_STATE = $CURR_STATE
   sleep 1
done
```

The preceding example is quite simple, but it can be made more useful by actually writing out the zone or zones that change by decoding the hex value that's returned by the i2cget command in the constituent zones.

In *Chapter 9, Putting It All Together*, you'll learn how this is done in order to display the individual status of each zone on a web page. You can use exactly the same technique to do this for your log files and, in fact, output to the log file by expanding on the same script.

Summary

In this chapter, we started off by learning how passive infrared sensors are used to detect motion to protect a predefined coverage area from intrusion. We then looked at connecting these to the inputs on our port expander via opto-couplers as we will now use 12V to power the alarm zone circuits.

We then looked at wireless alarm systems that operate on the open 433-MHz band, which is commonly used for security devices. After exploring the possibility of using the legacy 433-Util bit-banging software on our Raspberry Pi to decode the signals transmitted by devices using a simple receiver, we opted to use a paired receiver device that will interface easily with our alarm circuit inputs.

Finally, we created a simple script that will log the changes in our alarm inputs to a text file, which can later be expanded to log exactly what's going on with the system in detail.

6
Adding Cameras to Our Security System

Until now, we've been putting together the elements that will allow us to connect sensors to our alarm system to detect intrusions using either switches or passive infra-red motion detectors, which in turn will tell our Raspberry Pi that something has happened in a particular zone. These elements will all come together as a whole system later in this book.

Our system is now going to become a whole lot more sophisticated with the addition of cameras to take pictures and video clips, and e-mail them to us straightaway when it detects something.

We'll also use e-mail to send us alerts on our smart phone when we're out and about when any of the sensors in the system are triggered.

In this chapter we will cover the following topics:

- Setting up the Raspberry Pi camera module and learning how to capture stills and video images
- Learning how to overlay captured images with text and time-stamps
- Triggering image captures with a motion detector
- E-mailing the image and video files to us in real time
- Understanding the differences between capturing images during the day and during the night
- Switching on and off security lighting and other high-current devices when required
- Connecting a USB webcam instead of the native camera module

Prerequisites

You'll need the following parts for this chapter, on top of the components used in the previous chapter:

- A Raspberry Pi standard camera module
- A Raspberry Pi NoIR camera module
- An Infra-Red LED array and/or visible LED array
- A USB webcam

The Raspberry Pi camera module

The Raspberry Pi Camera Module is an official Raspberry Pi accessory that works with all models of the Pi, and can be used to take high-definition stills and video images. It connects directly to the Pi board's **camera serial interface** (CSI) port, which is dedicated to these modules to enable high-speed operation.

The camera itself is a 5 megapixel fixed-focus sensor supporting 1080p, 720p, and VGA video modes and still captures.

The official Raspberry Pi Camera Module

You can also obtain housings for the camera modules, which, unless you're going to build your own enclosure for the camera system, I recommend you use.

Raspberry Pi camera housings come in various colors and styles

Connecting the camera module

As previously mentioned, the module connects directly to the Raspberry Pi board via its dedicated camera interfaces, as shown in the following image. When connecting the camera, the contact side of the ribbon cable is toward the HDMI connector and the blue side of the cable is toward the network connector.

Connect the camera module to the dedicated interface

As you can see in the following image, the ribbon connector is not that long, so the camera needs to be located close to the Raspberry Pi. By using a camera enclosure, you could actually mount the camera directly on top of the Raspberry Pi case itself, if that works for you.

The camera module, housed within an enclosure

Setting up the camera module

Before we can use the camera module, we need to enable camera support on the Raspberry Pi. To do this, we use the `raspi-config` tool, as we did with the I2C bus earlier in our journey.

1. Connect to your Raspberry Pi the lazy way from your sofa using SSH, or directly using a keyboard and monitor.

2. Once you've logged in, launch the config tool with the following command:

```
$ sudo raspi-config
```

3. And then, select 5 Enable Camera.

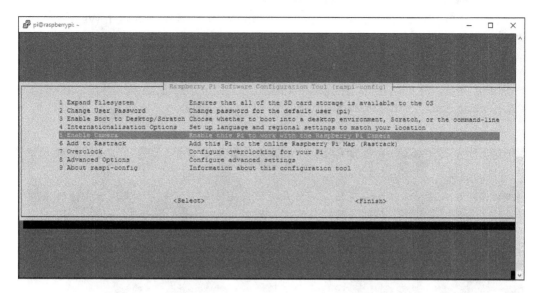

4. You'll then be asked to confirm whether you want to enable camera support.

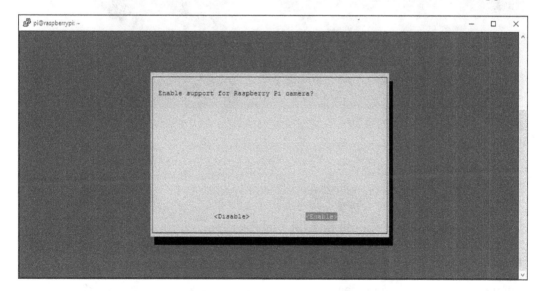

5. Select <Enable>.

6. Then, select **Finish** and reboot your Pi to enable the camera settings.

Testing the camera module

Once your Raspberry Pi has rebooted, your camera should be enabled. We can test this by taking a still image using the `raspistill` utility:

```
$ raspistill -v -o test.img
```

This will delay for 5 seconds then take a picture, while displaying various pieces of information, such as that shown in the following screenshot:

```
pi@raspberrypi ~ $ raspistill -v -o test.jpg

raspistill Camera App v1.3.8

Width 2592, Height 1944, quality 85, filename test.jpg
Time delay 5000, Raw no
Thumbnail enabled Yes, width 64, height 48, quality 35
Link to latest frame enabled   no
Full resolution preview No
Capture method : Single capture

Preview Yes, Full screen Yes
Preview window 0,0,1024,768
Opacity 255
Sharpness 0, Contrast 0, Brightness 50
Saturation 0, ISO 0, Video Stabilisation No, Exposure compensation 0
Exposure Mode 'auto', AWB Mode 'auto', Image Effect 'none'
Metering Mode 'average', Colour Effect Enabled No with U = 128, V = 128
Rotation 0, hflip No, vflip No
ROI x 0.000000, y 0.000000, w 1.000000 h 1.000000
Camera component done
Encoder component done
Starting component connection stage
Connecting camera preview port to video render.
Connecting camera stills port to encoder input port
Opening output file test.jpg
Enabling encoder output port
Starting capture 0
Finished capture 0
Closing down
Close down completed, all components disconnected, disabled and destroyed

pi@raspberrypi ~ $
```

 The camera module needs at least 128 MB of GPU memory to operate properly on Raspian. If you experience any issues, first ensure that the the `gpu_mem` setting in the `/boot/config.txt` configuration file is set to at least `128`.

And if all goes well, you should find the file, `test.jpg`, in your home folder. As you're connected via the shell, you wouldn't have seen the 5 second preview image displayed when the command was running.

If you download the image file to your PC, you should see a nice quality snap taken by the camera module.

The test photo taken by the Raspberry Pi Camera Module

 If you find that raspistill outputs errors when you run it, ensure that it is connected properly at both ends of the ribbon cable. One other catch is that sometimes the ribbon that connects the actual camera lens component to the tiny connector on the camera board can come loose. Just ensure that this is securely connected too. I've had this issue a couple times after the camera modules have been taken out of my box of random test bits to be used.

The `raspistill` utility has loads of options for manipulating the images it captures, and we'll use some of them a bit later in our capture script. In the meantime, to see the available options, run `raspistill` without any options and they will be listed:

```
$ raspistill
```

Be a video star

Now that we know our camera module is working, we can try and capture some video. To do this, we'll use the `raspivid` utility. The following command will take 5 seconds of high-definition video and save the file to your Raspberry Pi:

```
$ raspivid -o test.h264 -t 5000
```

You'll notice that file is called `test.h264` — this is because the video is captured as a raw **H.264** video stream. Unfortunately, not many media players will handle these files (although VLC player will — it rocks and handles practically anything you throw at it — get it on your PC at `www.videolan.org`).

If you want to play the file on smartphones and conventional media players, then we will need to wrap it in a container format, such as MPEG-4, and give the file a `.mp4` extension.

To do this, we'll use the **GPAC** package, which is an open source multimedia framework. It comes with a utility called **MP4Box**, which is a tool we'll use to create an MP4 container for our video file:

1. First, install the GPAC package:

    ```
    $ sudo apt-get install gpac
    ```

2. Once it's installed, run the command to convert the test video we created:

    ```
    $ MP4Box -fps 30 -add test.h264 test.mp4
    ```

You should now have the file, `test.mp4`, which you can download and play on your PC or smartphone.

> Another popular conversion tool is **ffmpeg**, which I use a lot on Windows to convert video files; however, it can be quite complex and although there is a package for the Raspberry Pi, I actually couldn't get it to convert properly on the Pi. MP4Box is much more straightforward and fitting for our needs.

Caught on camera

So, we now have a method of capturing still images and video, which we can put to use in our security system. If we want to have this running constantly, we could write a script to take video constantly, but this would soon fill up our memory card and wouldn't be particularly efficient. So, we'll combine our camera system with the motion detectors we connected earlier.

In the last chapter, we created an alarm zone which had a couple of sensors and a motion detector connected to our system on the input GPA0. So, let's write a script that will take a video clip whenever the motion detector is triggered:

```
#!/bin/bash


#set up port expander
sudo i2cset -y 1 0x20 0x00 0xFF

# loop forever
while true
```

```
do
  # read the GPA inputs
  GPA=$(sudo i2cget -y 1 0x20 0x12)

  # detect the zone on input 0
  if [ $GPA == "0x01" ]
  then
    #circuit normally closed so zone is OK
    #short delay
sleep 0.5

  else
    #zone is activated so take a 20 sec video clip

    #filename will be based on current timestamp
    sDate='date +%d%m%y'
    sTime='date +%T'
    echo "Zone 1 Activate at $sDate $sTime"

#take video clip
raspivid -o $sDate$sTime.h264 -t 20000

#convert to MP4
MP4Box -fps 30 -add $sDate$sTime.h264 $sDate$sTime.mp4
  fi
done
```

You have new mail

Having the images stored on your Raspberry Pi is not really much use—ideally, you would want the images sent to you straightaway, as soon as they are captured, so that you can view them on your smartphone.

An easy, quick, and reliable way to do this is to simply have them e-mailed to you. Hence we're going to add an e-mailing functionality to our home security system so that image captures are attached to a message and sent to your e-mail address straightaway, which you can access from your smartphone. The images can then be removed from your Raspberry Pi to prevent the SD card space from being clogged up with these reasonably large files.

Setting up the e-mail sender client

Fortunately, there are some good packages available that will help us with this. Carry out the following steps to install the email packages we need:

1. Update the package installer with the following command:

    ```
    $ sudo apt-get update
    ```

2. Install and set up the SMTP client with the following command:

    ```
    $ sudo apt-get install ssmtp
    ```

    You'll now need to set up the client to send emails through your email account. In the following configuration file, I've assumed that you have a Gmail account. The settings may be different if you use another email provider.

3. Open the `ssmtp` configuration file using **Nano** or another text editor:

    ```
    $ sudo nano /etc/ssmtp/ssmtp.conf
    ```

4. Replace the entries with the following configuration:

    ```
    root=<your-username>@gmail.com
    mailhub=smtp.gmail.com:587
    rewriteDomain=gmail.com
    AuthUser=<your-username>@gmail.com
    AuthPass=<your-password>
    FromLineOverride=YES
    UseSTARTTLS=YES
    ```

5. `ssmtp` can be used on its own but can be a bit of a faff while automatically sending emails (by default, you manually type the email in with the command line, or create a text file), so we're also going to install the `mailutils` package:

    ```
    $ sudo apt-get install mailutils
    ```

6. Once it's installed, we can use the `mail` command to send emails more easily. Send a test email through the (G)mail account that we set up earlier, using the following command to make sure your settings are working:

    ```
    $ echo "Test Email" | mail -s "Test Pi-Mail" me@mydomain.com
    ```

If all goes well, you should receive the test email in your mailbox within a few seconds or so.

Sending attachments

Now that we can send basic emails from our home security system, let's try sending the still image taken from our camera earlier. But first, we need to install yet another package to help us with this:

```
$ sudo apt-get install mpack
```

Once that's installed, you can send the test image file we took previously by using the following command:

```
$ sudo mpack -s "Security Photo" test.jpg me@mydomain.com
```

We now have all of the elements needed to send alerts and images from our home security system directly to our smartphone using email.

Where was that taken?

Ordinarily, you could just annotate the email message with where and when the attached image was taken, but that wouldn't be as cool as actually overlaying the image with some text, would it? So let's do some magic with the help of imagemagick, which is a popular command-line image manipulation tool. Install it with the following line:

```
$ sudo apt-get install imagemagick
```

We'll now use the command line to take the test photo that we took earlier, overlay some text using one of the imagemagick utilities, and save it to another file:

```
$ convert test.jpg -fill red -pointsize 48 annotate +20+60 'Camera 1'
annotated.jpg
```

After a few seconds, this will have generated a file called `annotated.jpg` containing our image with **Camera 1** written in red in the top corner. When we put all of this together in our final system, we'll also overlay the image with a time stamp.

 At the moment, the images generated by the `raspistill` tool are pretty large, being high resolution photos. This makes manipulating and sending them a bit time-consuming as far as processing time is concerned, so when we build our final system, we'll be using the `raspistill` options, -w, -h and, -q, to reduce the size and quality of the images to make the system more efficient.

To capture smaller image files, try using the following command:

```
$ raspistill -o test.img -h 768 -w 1024 -q 25
```

Night vision

The standard Raspberry Pi camera is great for taking daytime snaps of people walking up the garden path, but when it comes to night time shots, it's not really suitable. There are two ways of dealing with this: the first is to illuminate the capture area with a bright light when the PIR detector is triggered, and the second is to use the Raspberry Pi **NoIR camera module** and an infra-red LED array to let the camera see in the dark. More about that in a minute.

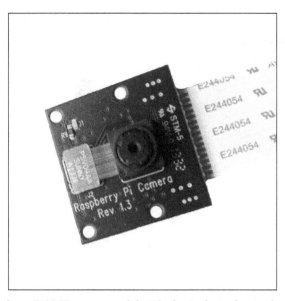

The Raspberry Pi NoIR camera module; it looks similar to the standard model

An illuminating experience

In order to switch on a light or LED array from the Raspberry Pi GPIO or our port expander circuit, we need something that will allow us to drive higher currents and voltages than can be provided by the GPIO ports alone.

A good candidate for this is the **TIP120 Darlington transistor**, which will allow us to switch on and off loads of up to 80V and 5 A from our GPIO pins. In our full system later on, we're going to use Port B of our MCP23017 port expander to control outputs, but the principle stands for any of the GPIO outputs available to us.

TIP120 transistors can be bought cheaply but can drive large loads

The following circuit shows how we can drive big loads from our GPIO port outputs.

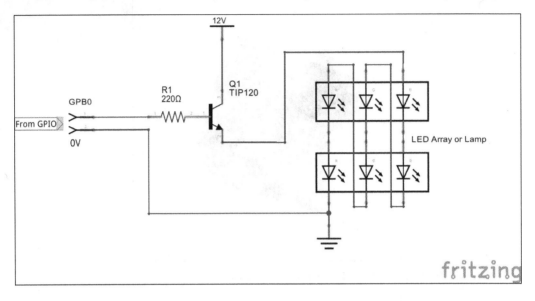

In our example circuit, we're using a GPIO output pin to control the base of our transistor via a 220 ohm resistor. When the GPIO pin goes high, the transistor is switched on and allows the 12V circuit to flow through the LED array.

In the preceding circuit, there is no current limiting for the LEDs because they are connected in series, and so with nine of them, each dropping about 1.5V across, this is about right for a 12V supply (yes I know I've only included six LEDs here but it's just for illustration). Remember to adjust for your particular needs. This circuit could easily drive other loads, such as bulbs or sounders.

 If you intend to drive high power loads, you will probably need to attach the TIP120 to a heat sink that will dissipate any heat and prevent it from over-heating and burning out. In our circuit that was demonstrated previously, however, you probably won't need one as we're only driving a couple of hundred milliwatts at most.

The Elaborate light switch re-visited

Expanding once again on our elaborate light switch from previous chapters, we can once again write a Bash script that will switch on our camera light, take a snap with the camera, and e-mail it to us when a PIR detector is triggered.

For the following script, we're assuming that the output controlling the TIP120 transistor is the Raspberry PI GPIO17 pin (D0 or pin 11 of our connector), which replaces the LED in our earlier set-up. The input from the PIR trigger is, again, connected to the GPA0 (port A, data pin 0) of our MCP23017 port expander. All the other inputs are tied low, as before, using 10 K resistors:

```bash
#!/bin/bash

#set up the High Load GPIO pin
sudo echo 17 > /sys/class/gpio/export
sudo echo out > /sys/class/gpio/gpio17/direction

#set up port expander Port A for inputs
sudo i2cset -y 1 0x20 0x00 0xFF

#clear the output by default to switch light off
sudo echo 0 > /sys/class/gpio/gpio17/value


# loop forever
while true
do
  # read the sensor state
  SWITCH=$(sudo i2cget -y 1 0x20 0x12)

  #PIR is normally closed so pin is held high
  if [ $SWITCH != "0x01" ]
  then
    #PIR was triggered - pin taken low

    #switch on lamp driver
    sudo echo 1 > /sys/class/gpio/gpio17/value
    sleep 0.5

#take a still image
    sudo raspistill -o -image.jpg -h 768 -w 1024 -q 25

    #email the image
    mpack -s "Security Alert Photo" test.jpg me@mydomain.com

    #switch off the lamp driver
    sudo echo 0 > /sys/class/gpio/gpio17/value
```

```
    fi
    #short delay
    sleep 0.5
  done
```

pir-camera-trigger.sh

You'll now see that we've started developing the foundations of the software that will control our home security system.

Is that a badger?

If you don't want to illuminate an area before capturing an image, you can use **infra-red lighting** in conjunction with a compatible camera. The standard Raspberry Pi camera module won't work with infra-red lighting because it contains an infra-red filter, but we can use the NoIR version of the camera module instead.

The Raspberry Pi NoIR camera module is exactly the same as the standard one, except that it doesn't have an infra-red filter built in, which means it will see in the dark with the aid of infra-red lighting. This makes it good for watching badgers at night as well as for use in our home security system.

You will need an infra-red LED array or cluster to invisibly illuminate the area you want to capture with the camera. These are readily available in various form factors and intensities, or you can build your own using individual infra-red LEDs purchased from an electronics store.

The Kingbright infra-red LED cluster runs from a 6V supply, which means you can connect two in series—one on either side of the camera.

Connecting and driving the LED cluster modules works exactly the same as our illuminating light above, using the TIP120 driver circuit. The only difference is that we humans can't see when the LEDs are on.

Using USB cameras

Instead of using the Raspberry Pi Camera Module, it's also possible to use a standard USB **webcam** to take still images. You should be aware though that the dedicated camera module is far superior to a USB webcam in terms of image quality. Although, you may already have a webcam knocking about in your box of bits, so why not try it?

Installing the webcam

After you've connected your webcam to a USB port on your Pi, you can check whether it's been recognized using the `lsusb` command:

```
$ lsusb
```

I'm using a Logitech webcam that gets reported as follows with `lsusb` (Device 006):

```
pi@raspberrypi ~ $ lsusb
Bus 001 Device 002: ID 0424:9514 Standard Microsystems Corp.
Bus 001 Device 001: ID 1d6b:0002 Linux Foundation 2.0 root hub
Bus 001 Device 003: ID 0424:ec00 Standard Microsystems Corp.
Bus 001 Device 006: ID 046d:08d8 Logitech, Inc. QuickCam for Notebook Deluxe
```

> Not all webcams will work with the Raspberry Pi. Even though it may be recognized as a USB device, it might not actually work properly with the operating system and create a video device (for example, `/dev/video0`). For example, an old cheap Trust webcam I had appeared as a USB device but wouldn't capture any images.
>
> You can check whether your webcam is likely to work with the Pi by checking your make and model at http://elinux.org/RPi_USB_Webcams.

So, now that the Pi knows that we have a webcam device attached, we can use the `fswebcam` utility to capture image frames. You can find out more about `fswebcam` from the developer's site at http://www.sanslogic.co.uk/fswebcam.

Install `fswebcam` with the following:

```
$ sudo apt-get install fswebcam
```

Taking a snap

You can now test the webcam by capturing a still image, which can be done by running the following command:

```
$ fswebcam test.jpg
```

You should expect to see output similar to the following:

```
pi@raspberrypi ~ $ lsusb
Bus 001 Device 002: ID 0424:9514 Standard Microsystems Corp.
Bus 001 Device 001: ID 1d6b:0002 Linux Foundation 2.0 root hub
Bus 001 Device 003: ID 0424:ec00 Standard Microsystems Corp.
Bus 001 Device 006: ID 046d:08d8 Logitech, Inc. QuickCam for Notebook Deluxe
pi@raspberrypi ~ $ fswebcam test.jpg
--- Opening /dev/video0...
Trying source module v4l2...
/dev/video0 opened.
No input was specified, using the first.
Adjusting resolution from 384x288 to 320x240.
--- Capturing frame...
Captured frame in 0.00 seconds.
--- Processing captured image...
Writing JPEG image to 'test.jpg'.
pi@raspberrypi ~ $
```

 fswebcam has lots of options for things like the resolution and quality of the image. Use the command fswebcam -? to get a list of all options.

Snap snap snap

fswebcam doesn't take video streams, but you can set it up to take a series of **frames** at regular intervals. For example, to take a snap every 10 seconds, you can use the following command:

```
$ fswebcam frame.jpg -l 10
```

An example of how this would be useful can be demonstrated by setting the webcam to take a snap every few seconds in the background (the -q switch runs fswebcam in the background). When our security system is triggered, we could then take the latest image snapped with the webcam which could be looking down your pathway.

For the purpose of putting together our entire system later in this book, we'll be focusing on the Raspberry Pi Camera Module, but you can always replace the code with the previous examples if you want to use USB webcams instead.

You'll notice that `fswebcam`, unlike `raspistill`, has the ability to overlay the images with timestamp information, so you don't need to worry about overlaying text as we did previously. Look at the `fswebcam` command line options for more information.

The multicamera setup

It may have occurred to you that the Raspberry Pi has only one camera module input. Now, this is obviously limiting if you want to have multiple cameras around your property that are triggered by motion detectors.

However, there is nothing stopping us from building standalone units that have a separate Raspberry Pi board with a PIR detector, Camera Module, and network connection, either using a Wi-Fi dongle or Ethernet.

Because you only need a single input to the Raspberry Pi to detect when the PIR motion sensor is triggered, you can use the on-board GPIO port to connect the sensor, rather than using a port expander. The Raspberry Pi will email the alert over the network, and could alert the main controller Pi if required — making it a slave sensor device.

You can readily obtain small PIR detectors, such as the Parallax one shown next, which you can mount onto a Raspberry Pi Case along with the camera module, creating a self-contained unit.

A Parallax PIR motion sensor (type 555-28027)

The Slave driver

While it may seem quite elaborate to have a Raspberry Pi for each camera—think about it—you can actually build each camera unit with all of the components for around £50, which is significantly cheaper than buying a wireless *smart* camera. If you really want to be clever, you could also use this as a slave device to accept further sensor inputs local to the unit.

There is nothing to stop you from connecting a GPIO output pin on the slave unit to drive an input on the main controller and control the pin depending on the state of its local sensors. By running a 6-core cable between the units, you could even power the slave unit if your power supply is man enough (you'd need to have a supply of 5V @ 1A for the slave Pi running along the wire).

I'm not going to go into any more detail about this configuration at this time, but you could set yourself a challenge to create a fully distributed home security system using multiple Raspberry Pis and the building blocks and concepts learned in this book.

Summary

In this chapter, we learned how to connect both Raspberry Pi camera modules and USB cameras to our Pi board in order to take image and video captures when required by our home security system. We also learned how to overlay our images with informative text and have the files immediately emailed to us.

In order to capture images from our camera at night, we also looked at ways to illuminate the capture area using both visible and infra-red lighting, with the ability to switch the lighting on and off as required by using a high-current Darlington transistor driver.

In the next chapter, we're going to get down to the business of putting together modules by building a mobile-optimized web-based control panel for our home security system. We'll learn how to set up a Web server on our Raspberry Pi and manipulate files using our Web control panel, which means that we'll start to explore how all of the elements we've encountered so far can come together as part of our final system.

7
Building a Web-Based
Control Panel

We've now got all of our hardware elements together for us to create a complete home-security system featuring contact switches for our doors and windows, and motion detectors and cameras to take happy snaps of wannabe intruders! I've deliberately guided you through this in a modular fashion so that you can pick and choose and expand on the hardware sensor elements that suit your requirements. In *Chapter 9*, *Putting It All Together* we will be wiring all of this together to form the complete system based on zones that we looked at earlier.

One thing that all home security systems require is a **control panel** that allows us to **arm** and **disarm** the system and monitor the status of the zones within our system. We might also want to do things such as only arm certain zones, or have the system automatically arm and disarm at certain times of the day.

The hardware required for this, such as switches, LEDs, and LCD displays, can be quite expensive and time-consuming to put together; they can also make the system less configurable and flexible. So, in our system, we're going to build a Web-based control panel that we can access from our mobile phone browser. This also means that we can control the system remotely, when we are out of the house.

In this chapter, we will cover the following:

- Defining the scope of our home security in terms of the number of zones we will be monitoring and the I/O ports we will use

- Learning how to install and configure a web server on our Raspberry Pi

- Developing a basic HTML5 web page for our alarm control panel

- Learning how to use PHP scripts to dynamically configure our system from the web page

Installing the web server

There are several **web servers** readily available that we could install on our Raspberry Pi, and they would all be suitable for our system. But I like the **lighttpd** web server as it's easy to use and lightweight. lighttpd is often referred to, and affectionately known as, "Lighty"—which to be honest is less of a mouthful than lighttpd.

As well as the Web server itself, we're also going to install **PHP** support, which will allow us to write dynamic web pages to interact with the Linux system. Now, to be honest, I'm not a massive fan of PHP for commercial Web-based deployments for many reasons, but for a small embedded-Linux system such as our home security system, it's perfect and works really well. It's also quite straightforward to get into if you've never done server-side Web-scripting as well.

To perform the following steps, you'll need to be logged into your Raspberry Pi via the terminal console (for example, PuTTY):

1. Update the package installer:

   ```
   $ sudo apt-get update
   ```

2. Install the `lighttpd` Web server:

   ```
   $ sudo apt-get install lighttpd
   ```

   Once installed, it will automatically start up as a background service, and will do so each time your Raspberry Pi starts up.

3. Install PHP5 support:

   ```
   $ sudo apt-get install php5-cgi
   ```

4. Now, we need to enable the PHP FastCGI module in our web server:

   ```
   $ sudo lighty-enable-mod fastcgi-php
   ```

5. And finally, we need to restart the Web server:

   ```
   $ sudo /etc/init.d/lighttpd
   ```

That's it! You should now have your PHP Web server installed. By default, the web content files get installed in the location, /var/www, and Lighty installs a test placeholder page in this location, which you can access from your browser by simply entering the IP address of your Raspberry Pi, as shown in the following screenshot:

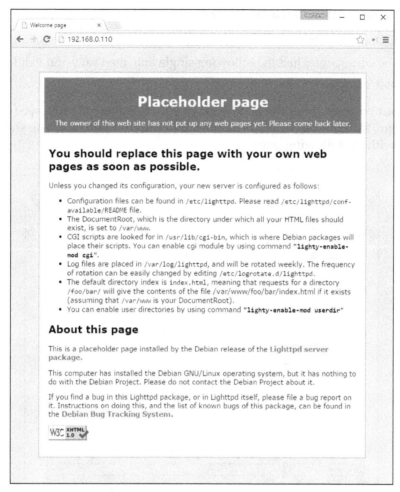

The Lighttpd placeholder page

Testing the PHP5 installation

While we're at it, we should also test our PHP installation, as this is fundamental to building our console. This can be done by writing a simple PHP script page that, if PHP is installed correctly, will return information about its environment and configuration:

1. First, go to the web content folder:

    ```
    $ cd /var/www
    ```

2. In Nano, create a file called `phpinfo.php`:

    ```
    $ sudo nano phpinfo.php
    ```

3. In the editor, enter just the following single line, then save and exit from Nano:

    ```
    <?php phpinfo(); ?>
    ```

Now, in your browser, enter the IP address of your Raspberry Pi followed by / `phpinfo.php`, for example, http://192.168.0.110/phpinfo.php, and you should be presented with the following page:

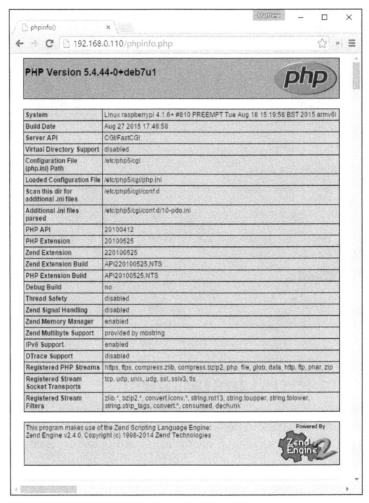

The PHP info page generated by the Web server

Now that we know our web server is working properly, we can start creating our console web page.

Being in control

So that we know what controls we want on our alarm control panel, we need to map out our system with the number of zone inputs and control inputs and outputs. As you'll remember from *Chapter 3, Extending Your Pi to Connect More Things* we can essentially have up to 16 zones in our system using the two I/O ports on our port expander. We also have the eight GPIO pins at our disposal on the Raspberry Pi board itself. So, let's now allocate these outputs and document them in the table that follows.

I'm going to set up an 8-zone system for my alarm inputs using port A on the I/O expander board, using the native GPIO pins for things such as buttons and alert outputs. One reason for doing it in this configuration is that the system can always fail-safe—so if the expander board fails, the Raspberry Pi can still communicate alerts and buzzers connected to it.

Port	I/O Pin	Label/Purpose
Expander A	0 (A0)	Zone 1 Input (Entry/Exit Channel)
	1 (A1)	Zone 2 Input
	2 (A2)	Zone 3 Input
	3 (A3)	Zone 4 Input
	4 (A4)	Zone 5 Input
	5 (A5)	Zone 6 Input
	6 (A6)	Zone 7 Input
	7 (A7)	Zone 8 – Anti-Tamper Loop Input
Expander B	0 (B0)	
	1 (B1)	
	2 (B2)	
	3 (B3)	
	4 (B4)	
	5 (B5)	
	6 (B6)	
	7 (B7)	
R-Pi GPIO	0 (GP0)	Arm/Disarm Switch (Input)
	1 (GP1)	
	2 (GP2)	
	3 (GP3)	
	4 (GP4)	Armed LED (Output)

Port	I/O Pin	Label/Purpose
	5 (GP5)	Arm/Disarm Buzzer (Output)
	6 (GP6)	Alarm LED (Output)
	7 (GP7)	Alarm Bell (Output)

Arming yourself

The terms *arm* and *disarm* are alarm system-speak for switching the alarm monitoring on (**arming** the system) and off (**disarming** the system). Zone 1 of our system is going to be linked to the arming and disarming part of the system as it will be connected to the sensors on the door that we leave or enter from; this will be a special zone for **entry** or **exit** purposes.

When we set the alarm, we need a bit of time to get out of the house. The way that the system knows we've left the property is by monitoring the *exit* zone to see if we've opened and then closed the front door behind us within the time allowed.

Similarly, when we return, we will open the front door, but we don't want the alarm to go off straightaway—we need a chance to disarm the system within a given amount of time. We will arm and disarm the system via our web-based control panel, or by using a switch of some sort on the input GP0.

The master configuration file

Our system will use a **master configuration file** that will tell it how everything is set up and connected. This configuration file will be used by both the web control panel and the main alarm control scripts so that the two sub-systems can "talk" to each other. Let's create the file with our initial settings.

The settings file will be stored in the same location as where we will create our control scripts in *Chapter 9, Putting It All Together*, which is in the folder. /etc/pi-alarm. So, let's create this folder, and give it execute rights so that our scripts can be run:

```
$ cd /etc
$ sudo mkdir pi-alarm
$ sudo chmod 777 pi-alarm
```

We'll now create the master configuration file, to be used by our system, in this folder:

```
$ cd pi-alarm
$ sudo nano alarm.cfg
```

As before, you don't have to create your files in Nano on the Raspberry Pi—you can create them on your desktop computer, and then transfer them to your Pi using SCP.

```
# ALARM MASTER CONFIG FILE #

#Number of zones in the system
NUM_ZONES=8

#Display labels for each zone
ZONE_LABEL_1="Zone 1 - Entry/Exit"
ZONE_LABEL_2="Zone 2"
ZONE_LABEL_3="Zone 3"
ZONE_LABEL_4="Zone 4"
ZONE_LABEL_5="Zone 5"
ZONE_LABEL_6="Zone 6"
ZONE_LABEL_7="Zone 7"
ZONE_LABEL_8="Zone 8"

#Zones that are enabled
#Set to 0 to Disable or 1 to Enable
ZONE_ENABLE_1=1
ZONE_ENABLE_2=1
ZONE_ENABLE_3=1
ZONE_ENABLE_4=1
ZONE_ENABLE_5=1
ZONE_ENABLE_6=1
ZONE_ENABLE_7=1
ZONE_ENABLE_8=1

SYSTEM_ARMED=0

#Zone status
#Set to 1 if zone is triggered
ZONE_STATUS_1=0
ZONE_STATUS_2=0
ZONE_STATUS_3=0
ZONE_STATUS_4=0
ZONE_STATUS_5=0
ZONE_STATUS_6=0
ZONE_STATUS_7=0
ZONE_STATUS_8=0
```

`alarm.cfg` file

Creating the web page

Our Web-based control panel is going to be a single PHP-driven HTML5 web page which will be **mobile optimized**. HTML5 is the latest mark-up standard for web pages and is supported by most modern smartphones and browsers. We will also create a **cascading style-sheet** (**CSS**) that will make our page look half reasonable on mobile devices.

To create the web files, I recommend that you use something like the excellent Notepad++ on your desktop computer, rather than doing it directly on the Raspberry Pi. Alternatively, if you are a seasoned web developer, you may already have your IDE of choice.

The control panel HTML template

The first thing we'll do is create an HTML file that we can use to test our layout before we put the HTML into a PHP file to make it interact with our system. This makes it easier to tweak the way we want it to look beforehand, without the PHP scripts getting in the way.

 This is not a tutorial on Web development—there is a plethora of books out there on that subject—but I hope the code is clear enough for you to work out what's going on. The code I'm going to show you is fully functional, so you can just use what I give you without having to do any more. Hopefully, it makes your control panel look OK too!

The following mark-up gives you a basic control panel with status for our 8 zones, a master arm and disarm switch, and switches to enable or disable any of our zones.

The `<head>` section of the code contains some `<meta>` tags that help mobile devices know that it's a mobile-friendly site. In the main `<body>` mark-up, we have a section for each zone that contains the zone's name and an on/off switch. Each zone is in its container so that we can also highlight a particular zone that needs our attention, for example, if it's triggered.

You can find the full HTML5 markup for our control panel in the `alarm-panel.html` file located inside the code folder of `chapter 7`.

Giving it some style

At the moment, this page doesn't look that great (in fact, it looks awful, like something from the 1990s); it isn't particularly good for mobile devices and would most certainly fail the *sausage test*. So, we're going to apply some styling to make it look not half bad. Although the preceding mark-up contains a reference to a CSS file — we haven't created that file — so this is what our page currently looks like (as I said: it looks awful):

The web control panel without any styling

The following CSS3 mark-up is designed specifically for our control panel, and it makes it look quite nice while also making it usable on **touch-screen** mobile devices. The CSS is quite long and seems overwhelming, but you don't need to do anything with it, or understand it, if you don't want to — the only thing you need to know is that it's been designed for modern browsers and smartphones, so don't expect it to work on Internet Explorer 7, or probably even IE9!

In essence, it contains the styling for the following:

- Preparing the browser for our mobile layout
- Our text and zone areas
- Creating cool switches instead of boring checkboxes
- Making an area flash on and off when we need it to

```css
/* Clear browser margin and padding defaults */
body, div, dl, dt, dd, ul, ol, li, h1, h2, h3, h4, h5, h6, pre, form,
fieldset, input, textarea, p {
margin:0;padding:0;-webkit-text-size-adjust:none;
}

body {
  background: #ffffff;
  color: #4A5651;
  font-family: "Trebuchet MS", Helvetica, sans-serif;
  font-size:10px;
  height: 100%;
  padding:0;
  margin:0 auto;
  max-width:320px;
  min-width:240px;
  text-align: left;
  width:100%;
  -webkit-box-shadow: 0px 20px 40px 0px rgba(0,0,0,0.50);
  -moz-box-shadow: 0px 20px 40px 0px rgba(0,0,0,0.50);
  box-shadow: 0px 20px 40px 0px rgba(0,0,0,0.50);
}

p, .zoneLabel {
  font-size:16px;
  margin:5px;
  line-height:1.4;
  color:#4A5651;
}

#header h1 {
  font-size:20px;
  line-height:40px;
  margin:0;
  padding:0 0 0 15px;
  text-align:center;
```

```
    text-overflow: ellipsis;
    font-weight:bold;
}

.zoneControl, .masterControl{
  border-bottom:1px solid #dddddd;
  margin-top:5px;
  margin-bottom:0px;
  padding:5px;
  display:block;
  width:100%;
}

.zoneLabel {
  font-weight:bold;
  text-overflow:ellipsis;
}

input[type="submit"] {
  border: none;
  background-color: #0b70cc;
  color: white;
  height: 32px;
  display: block;
  padding: 4px 7px;
  float: left;
  border-radius: 8px;
  position: relative;
  bottom: 1px;
  margin-left: 4px;
  text-align: center;
}
input[type="submit"]:hover {background-color: #b2ceec;color:
#0b70cc;border: none;border: 1px solid #b2ceec;}

/* Flashing animation */
@-webkit-keyframes flash{0%, 50%, 100% {opacity: 1;} 25%, 75%
{opacity: 0;}}
@keyframes flash {0%, 50%, 100% {opacity: 1;} 25%, 75% {opacity: 0;}}
.flash {
  -webkit-animation-name:
  flash;animation-name:
  flash;color:#f00000;
}
```

```css
.animated {
  -webkit-animation-duration: 1s;
  animation-duration: 1s;
  -webkit-animation-fill-mode: both;
  animation-fill-mode: both;
  animation-iteration-count:infinite;
  -webkit-animation-iteration-count:infinite;
}

/*
  ON/OFF SWITCH STYLES
  The rather cool On/Off switch styling was generated on
  https://proto.io/freebies/onoff/
*/
.onoffswitch {
  position: relative;
  width: 90px;
  -webkit-user-select: none;
  -moz-user-select: none;
  -ms-user-select: none;
}

.onoffswitch-checkbox {
  display: none;
}

.onoffswitch-label {
  display: block;
  overflow: hidden;
  cursor: pointer;
  border: 2px solid #FFFFFF;
  border-radius: 20px;
}

.onoffswitch-inner {
  display: block;
  width: 200%;
  margin-left: -100%;
  transition: margin 0.3s ease-in 0s;
}

  .onoffswitch-inner:before, .onoffswitch-inner:after {
    display: block;
    float: left;
```

```
    width: 50%;
    height: 30px;
    padding: 0;
    line-height: 30px;
    font-size: 14px;
    color: white;
    font-family: Trebuchet, Arial, sans-serif;
    font-weight: bold;
    box-sizing: border-box;
  }

  .onoffswitch-inner:before {
    content: "ON";
    padding-left: 10px;
    background-color: #34C290;
    color: #FFFFFF;
  }

  .onoffswitch-inner:after {
    content: "OFF";
    padding-right: 10px;
    background-color: #EEEEEE;
    color: #999999;
    text-align: right;
  }

.onoffswitch-switch {
  display: block;
  width: 18px;
  margin: 6px;
  background: #FFFFFF;
  position: absolute;
  top: 0;
  bottom: 0;
  right: 56px;
  border: 2px solid #FFFFFF;
  border-radius: 20px;
  transition: all 0.3s ease-in 0s;
}

.onoffswitch-checkbox:checked + .onoffswitch-label .onoffswitch-inner
{
  margin-left: 0;
}
```

```css
.onoffswitch-checkbox:checked + .onoffswitch-label .onoffswitch-switch
{
  right: 0px;
}

.masterswitch {
  position: relative;
  width: 90px;
  -webkit-user-select: none;
  -moz-user-select: none;
  -ms-user-select: none;
}

.masterswitch-checkbox {
  display: none;
}

.masterswitch-label {
  display: block;
  overflow: hidden;
  cursor: pointer;
  border: 2px solid #FFFFFF;
  border-radius: 20px;
}

.masterswitch-inner {
  display: block;
  width: 200%;
  margin-left: -100%;
  transition: margin 0.3s ease-in 0s;
}

.masterswitch-inner:before, .masterswitch-inner:after {
  display: block;
  float: left;
  width: 50%;
  height: 30px;
  padding: 0;
  line-height: 30px;
  font-size: 12px;
  color: white;
  font-family: Trebuchet, Arial, sans-serif;
  font-weight: bold;
  box-sizing: border-box;
```

```
}

.masterswitch-inner:before {
  content: "ARMED";
  padding-left: 10px;
  background-color: #F00000;
  color: #FFFFFF;
}

.masterswitch-inner:after {
  content: "OFF";
  padding-right: 10px;
  background-color: #EEEEEE;
  color: #999999;
  text-align: right;
}

.masterswitch-switch {
  display: block;
  width: 18px;
  margin: 6px;
  background: #FFFFFF;
  position: absolute;
  top: 0;
  bottom: 0;
  right: 56px;
  border: 2px solid #FFFFFF;
  border-radius: 20px;
  transition: all 0.3s ease-in 0s;
}

.masterswitch-checkbox:checked + .masterswitch-label .masterswitch-inner {
  margin-left: 0;
}

.masterswitch-checkbox:checked + .masterswitch-label .masterswitch-switch {
  right: 0px;
}
/* END OF SWITCH STYLES */
```

Web control panel style sheet – `alarm-panel.css`

Apply the stylesheet and this is what you end up with (a little bit nicer, I think you'll agree):

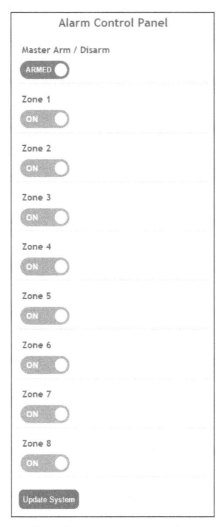

The web control panel with styling

Making it dynamic

Now that we have the layout code defined for our control panel page, we can insert it in our PHP page so that it can be modified dynamically by the PHP script on the Web server, depending on the status of our home security system.

The PHP script will help us achieve the following basic functions:

- Updating the configuration file with the position of the on/off switches for zones

- Arming and disarming the system

- Telling us which zone has been triggered when an intrusion has been detected

Again, I'm not going to go into detail about how the PHP code works, but hopefully the comments within the code will help you follow what's going on, and also help you modify it if you want to change its behavior.

Getting a bit of help first

Unless you change some of the PHP configuration, it can be a nightmare trying to work out what's gone wrong if you have a small bug in your code, as basically you are presented with...nothing!

So, before we create and build our PHP page, we'll change a couple of settings in the PHP configuration file to make sure we know if there are any issues:

1. Open the configuration file with **Nano**:

   ```
   $ sudo nano /etc/php5/cgi/php.ini
   ```

2. The file is a bit large and unwieldy, but battle your way through it, find these settings, and change them as follows:

   ```
   error_reporting = E_ALL
   ```

   ```
   display_errors = On
   ```

3. Save the file and exit Nano.

4. Finally, restart Lighty:

   ```
   $ sudo /etc/init.d/lighttpd restart
   ```

The main PHP code

And here it is... But don't run it yet—there's still a bit more to do...

You can find the full main PHP code in the `index.php` file located inside the code folder of `chapter 7`. In our Web server content folder, we should now have the following files:

```
pi@raspberrypi ~ $ ls -1 /var/www
alarm-panel.css
alarm-panel.html
index.lighttpd.html
index.php
phpinfo.php
```

I'm someone else

Now, before we can actually open this PHP web page successfully, we need to be aware of the fact that the Web server, by default, actually runs as a different user called `www-data`. This means that it doesn't ordinarily have the right to perform certain operations; in particular, those that interact with the file system.

If you worked through the previous PHP script, you'll see that it actually executes some Linux commands to read and update our `alarm.cfg` file.

In the same way that we have to put `sudo` in front of many commands because we're not the root user, it is true for other users as well, including `www-data`. So, to give the Web server rights to execute certain commands, we need to add it as a **sudoer**, using the **visudo** utility.

Run the utility to open the sudoer configuration file:

$ sudo visudo

At the bottom of the file, add the following line:

```
www-data ALL=(ALL) NOPASSWD:/bin/cat,/etc/pi-alarm/update-alarm-
setting.sh
```

Then save the file and exit.

The final thing we have to do is create a small **Bash script** that will handle the task of updating settings in our `alarm.cfg` file. The reason why we need to do this is because we're going to use the Linux `sed` command to update the file. The way that we are invoking the `sed` command means that it needs to create a temporary file. Unless we do a bit of work with configuring the Web server because of its file location context, it won't work. So, it's easier to create a stub Bash script that is called by the PHP script. In this way, the Bash environment deals with the temporary file context.

So, we'll create the following Bash script and save it in our `/etc/pi-alarm` folder:

```
#!/bin/bash
#/etc/pi-alarm/update-alarm-setting.sh
###########################################
# Provides access to the sed command from  #
# PHP as it needs write access to a temp    #
# folder.                                   #
# $1 - Setting Name                         #
# $2 - Setting Value                        #
###########################################

sed -i "s/^\($1\s*= *\).*/\1$2/" /etc/pi-alarm/alarm.cfg
```

update-alarm-setting.sh

And then we need to give the script execution rights:

`$ sudo chmod 777 /etc/pi-alarm/update-alarm-setting.sh`

This is what we should see in our `/etc/pi-alarm` folder at this time:

```
pi@raspberrypi ~ $ ls -1 /etc/pi-alarm
alarm.cfg
update-alarm-setting.sh
```

Right, after all that, I think we can now launch the control panel page in our browser at

`http://<my-pi-ip>.`

`index.php` is configured as a default page in Lighty's config, so you don't need to add it to the end of the URL; just the IP address will suffice.

By changing the switch positions and then clicking on the **Update System** button, you should find that the setting values get updated accordingly in `alarm.cfg`. You can now see how this file will be the way for the status to be exchanged between our web console and the security system scripts that we'll develop in *Chapter 9, Putting It All Together*.

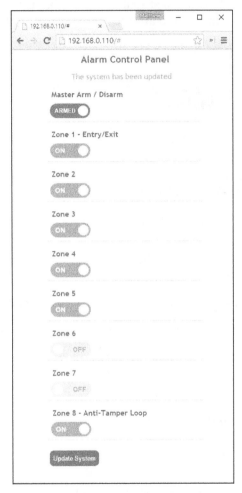

The final operational control panel

Remote access to our control panel

While we can set up our system to receive email alerts when our system detects an intrusion, it would be really useful to be able to access our Web-based control panel wherever we are so that we can perhaps arm and disarm the system or switch off certain zones when we're not there.

However, in order to make this possible we need to do a few things:

Setting up a dynamic DNS account

Most of us won't have a **fixed IP address** for the Internet connection in our home; it is likely to change from time to time, especially when we reboot or unplug our router, whereby our Internet service provider assigns us a new one when we next connect to them. Because of this, we can't rely on using the IP address to get to our home network when we're out and about. To solve this, we need to set up a **dynamic DNS** account that will allow us to set up a domain name for our home network (for example, *myhomenetwork.com*).

It works by having a service that runs inside your network, such as on your router or laptop, that updates the dynamic DNS service hosting your domain name with the current IP address of your Internet connection. Then, when you use your domain name in your browser, it will take you to a Web server on your home network.

Popular dynamic DNS providers out there include No-IP (www.noip.com) and DynDNS (www.dyn.com). You can also get a free DnsOMatic account with OpenDNS to manage your services (www.dnsomatic.com).

My Netgear NAS device has a DnsOMatic updater service add-on

My Netgear Router has the option of updating a Dynamic DNS service

The Raspberry Pi dynamic DNS client

Since your Raspberry Pi-based home security system is likely to always be on, you might want to install the **ddclient** updater service on there instead:

```
$ sudo apt-get install ddclient
```

Once installed, you can set it up for your particular service and account details using the following config file:

```
$ sudo nano /etc/ddclient.conf
```

Setting up a static IP on your Raspberry Pi

So that our home network always knows where to find your Raspberry Pi, we need to set up a **static IP address** on it, assuming that it currently acquires an IP address from your router's DHCP server each time it boots up.

1. To do this, we need to edit the network settings on the Raspberry Pi. In Nano, open the following configuration file:

   ```
   $ sudo nano /etc/network/interfaces
   ```

2. You'll probably find the Ethernet port configuration set to something like this:

auto eth0

allow-hotplug eth0

iface eth0 inet manual

3. Change this configuration to be an unused static IP address on your network. In my case, I've set it to 192.168.0.99. The gateway setting is the IP address of my Internet router:

```
auto eth0
allow-hotplug eth0
iface eth0 inet static
        address 192.168.0.99
        netmask 255.255.255.0
        gateway 192.168.0.1
```

4. Now, we need to restart the networking service — note that you'll be disconnected from your terminal session. You'll need to reconnect using the new IP address:

$ sudo /etc/init.d/networking restart

If you have any issues, simply restart the Pi with sudo reboot and all should be good when it comes back up.

Port-forwarding

The final piece of this puzzle is to make sure that our Internet router will direct incoming traffic on a given port to our Raspberry Pi's Web server. For the purpose of this example, I'm going to assume that we are going to stick to the default, port 80, on our Web server.

A word about security

Given that our Web server will now be accessible from the outside world, we need to be mindful about securing our system properly. The two main ways to do this are to change the Web server port to a random number other than 80 (for example, 8799) and add password protection to your site by applying basic authentication. Both of these can be done in the lighttpd configuration file.

Most routers will allow you to set up **port-forwarding** as part of their **firewall** configuration. Essentially, setting this means that any incoming traffic from the Internet on a given TCP port will be allowed to pass through the router and will be directed to the device with the specified IP address. On my Netgear router, it's set up as shown in the following screenshot:

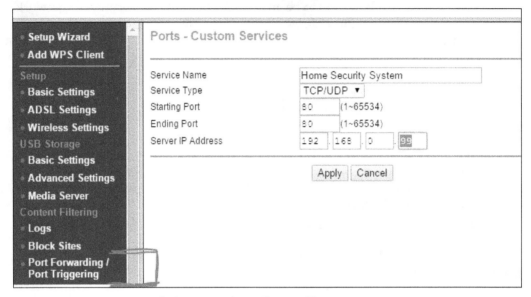

Setting up port-forwarding on a Netgear router

Now, when you enter your personal domain name in your browser, when you're away from home you should be taken to your alarm control panel.

You might also want to consider opening up port 22 so that you can access the Raspberry Pi directly using PuTTy and SSH from outside your network.

Summary

We've now started building the software that will control our home security system by determining the format of the main configuration file. We've also installed a Web server and built a basic single-page control panel with PHP, HTML5, and CSS3, which can be accessed nicely on our mobile phone, allowing us to configure our system and view the status.

In addition, we've learned how to configure our home network and Raspberry Pi so that we can access our control panel when we're away from home.

In *Chapter 9, Putting It All Together*, we'll put all of the electronic elements together and write the main scripts that will run the home security system. But before that, in the next chapter, we're going to look at a few other bits and pieces, such as adding other sensors, not necessarily related to intruder detection, to our home security system. We'll also look at how we can administer our entire Raspberry Pi system remotely using a Web browser, in addition to accessing our home security control panel.

8

A Miscellany of Things

The previous chapters have provided us with the foundation and elements to design and put together our entire home security system, which we will do in the next chapter. I hope that I've guided you through this journey in a fairly structured and logical way so that you are ready to do that.

Beforehand, though, I'm including this chapter dubbed a *Miscellany of Things*, as that's exactly what it is. It comprises a few optional, but useful, extras that we should consider for our system, but that don't really warrant a whole chapter in their own right. I guess you could refer to them as footnotes to previous chapters.

As such, we will take a look at the following topics:

- Ways to arm and disarm the system without the web-based panel
- Driving inductive loads safely from our GPIO outputs
- Adding an escaped water sensor input to our system
- Adding a temperature sensor input to our system
- How carbon monoxide detectors could be added to our system
- Remotely managing our Raspberry Pi using Webmin

Arming and disarming the system

We've included a switch on our Web-based control panel so that you can arm and disarm the system from your smartphone. However, this is probably not the most convenient way of doing it, especially when you're rushing out of the house, or you've returned home with a phone whose battery is flat. So, we need to find an additional way of arming and disarming our system at the entry and exit point of our property.

In the zone list table in the previous chapter, you'll notice that I assigned input GP0 on the Raspberry Pi GPIO as our arm/disarm switch input. This input will work in conjunction with our control panel switch.

This input can as be a simple as a toggle switch, or a bit more secure, such as a **key switch** or **electronic keypad**. Either way, it will be wired to ground GP0 (GPIO17) on our Raspberry Pi when the system is armed.

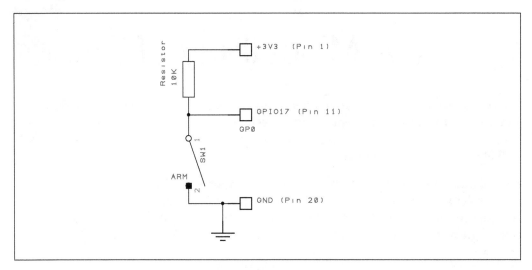

The circuit diagram for our arm/disarm switch

If you have switches or other such devices that will be outside and exposed to the elements, you'll need to ensure that they are suitable for outdoor use so that they don't get damaged and compromise the integrity of the system.

The IP67-rated key switch, suitable for outdoor use (type Lorlin WRL-5-E-S-2-B)

By using a standalone **security keypad**, you can allow each user to have their own code to arm and disarm the system. For example, the CDVI ECO 100 is a low-cost keypad that allows up to a 100 users. When the correct code is entered, it will arm the system by closing an internal switch. When the code is entered again, the keypad will disarm the system by opening the switch.

The CDVI ECO 100 programmable keypad

Driving inductive loads

I talked about driving large loads in *Chapter 6, Adding Cameras to Our Security System*, but now is probably a good time to expand on this a bit and talk about driving **inductive loads** such as **bells** and incandescent **lamps**. In the previous circuit example, I used the TIP120 Darlington transistor to drive an LED array that was not inductive. With inductive loads, you need to add a bit of diode protection to protect the circuit against spikes generated by the coils within relays and bells as they switch on and off.

Here's the modified circuit for our digital load driver with a 1N4007 **rectifier diode** for protection:

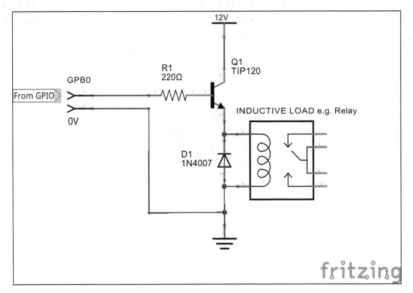

The digital load driver with diode protection

Beyond intrusion

Home security is not just about protecting our property against intrusion, it's also about protecting against other risks too, such as flood, fire, carbon monoxide leaks, and so on. So, it makes sense to extend our home security system to detect these other risks too.

You may choose to set up the system so that certain types of alerts only come to your phone as emails, rather than triggering all of the outside bells, lights, and whistles. This can be done by adapting the scripts in the next chapter so that they operate how you want them to.

A simple water detector

There's nothing worse than being away for a few days and coming home to a flooded kitchen because a leak has developed under the sink. Our simple circuit will detect the presence of water and trigger an input on our home security system, which can then alert you. You can also buy kits and ready-built modules to do this, but the following circuit is cheap and features our opto-isolator as we're going to have a different voltage for our actual detector.

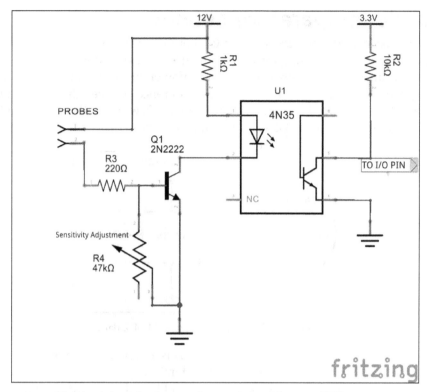

The circuit for a simple water detector, isolated from our GPIO input

How it works

When water is placed across the probes, current flows through the water, and so, through the R3/R4 potential divider on the base of transistor Q1. When the current at the base is high enough to saturate it, the transistor will switch on fully, allowing the LED inside the opto-coupler to switch on. This in turn will pull down the input pin to our system to ground via the photo-transistor inside the optocoupler.

You can use the trimmer, R4, to calibrate the sensor by adjusting its sensitivity. Any generic NPN bipolar transistor should work here, but obviously, they all have different operating parameters, so choose a suitable one.

A simple temperature sensor

If we want to be alerted when the ambient temperature reaches a certain threshold, then we can build a circuit using the commonly used LM34/LM35 temperature sensors. It's a simple device with just three pins: power, ground, and output, providing a voltage proportional to the temperature. The difference between the LM34 and LM35 is that the LM34 produces an output of 10mV/°F, whereas the LM35 produces 10mV/°C. There is also an LM335 variant that produces an output of 100mV/°K.

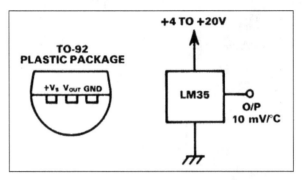

Pinout taken from the Texas Instruments LM35DZ datasheet

It may have occurred to you at this point that this is an analogue device—so how do we interface that with our wholly digital system? One way is to incorporate an analogue-to-digital interface onto our input control board and read the data coming in from that so that we know the exact temperature, but that's probably a bit beyond the scope of this book. So, we're going to implement a circuit that will alert us when the temperature exceeds a pre-defined threshold, which is probably all we need in the context of our home security system.

If you're interested in building an analogue-to-digital module to extend your home security, then take a look at something such as the PCF8591 chip from NXP, which is an I2C-based analogue-to-digital converter. This will connect to the I2C bus that we're already using, and so it is effectively just an add-on.

`http://bit.ly/NXPPCF8591`

For our temperature detector circuit, we will use an operational amplifier configured as a comparator that will trigger our opto-coupler input when the pre-set temperature is reached. So, for fire detection, we might want to detect when the ambient temperature has exceeded 50°C.

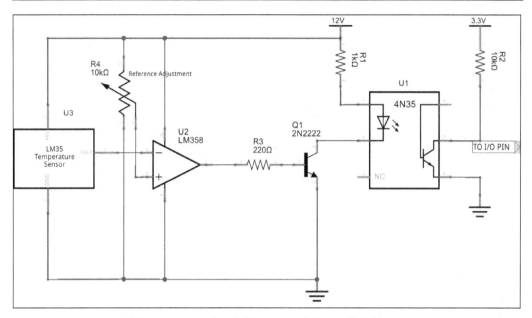

The temperature threshold sensor to drive our digital input

How it works

The reference voltage is set by the variable resistor, R4, which forms a voltage divider between the 12V and the ground. This essentially means that the reference voltage on the +ve input of the op-amp comparator can be between 0 and 12V. Assuming that we want to detect when 50° is reached, we will need the op-amp to trigger when the –ve is 500mV (10mV/°C).

In our circuit, the output of the op-amp is high in its normal state, which keeps the opto-coupler on. However, when the threshold is reached, the output of the op-amp is driven low, switching off the transistor Q1, and hence, the opto-coupler. This pulls our alarm input high via resistor R2.

A carbon monoxide detector

It's entirely possible to build smoke and carbon-monoxide detectors that we can connect to our home security system in a similar way to the previous sensors, although they are a little bit more complex as they can require special handling. The SparkFun MQ-7 **Carbon Monoxide (CO)** detector (which is actually made by Winsen Electronics) can be implemented in a similar way to our temperature sensor, triggering an alarm input when a particular threshold is reached.

The Winsen MQ-7 carbon monoxide gas detector, available from SparkFun.

The maximum safe continuous exposure to carbon monoxide (CO) is 9ppm (parts-per-million) according to ASHRAE (www.ashrae.org), and you should certainly not be exposed to CO higher than this for prolonged periods of time, with 35ppm being the absolute maximum for a normal 8-hour working day.

The MQ-7 detector has a sensitivity of between 10 and 500ppm, so in my mind, I'd want to be alerted as soon as it picks up anything, therefore we should set our comparator's reference voltage to the lower end of the scale, in accordance with the sensitivity curve taken from the datasheet, shown as follows:

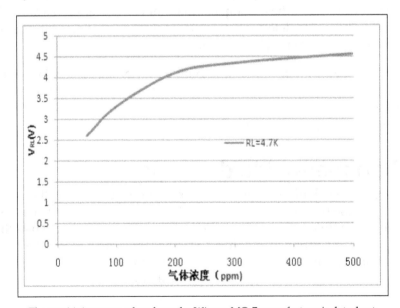

The sensitivity curve taken from the Winsen MQ-7 manufacturer's datasheet.

Warning

I've included this section on carbon monoxide detection more for interest than anything else. It's nasty stuff, and while rolling out your own detector is OK for interest's sake, please keep it just for that. It's useful to have this in our home security system to alert us when we're out of the house as an addition, but this *should not* be a replacement for a commercially available one that sits next to your boiler with all of the certifications, standards, and so on, and makes a very loud noise when we're in the house.

Remote administration for our Raspberry Pi

In the previous chapter, we learned how to set up our system and home network so that we can remotely access the alarm control panel from wherever we are. I'm now going to show you how to extend this to be able to administer and monitor our entire Raspberry Pi system.

Getting Webmin

Webmin is a rather fine and well established web-based interface for administering Unix/Linux systems. You can find everything about Webmin on its website at www. webmin.com. I'm assuming, as throughout this book, that you are using the Raspbian distribution on our Pi when it comes to installing Webmin.

There are a couple of ways to install Webmin: either by manually downloading and unpacking it, or by updating our repository sources so that we can use apt-get. I'm going to opt for the latter, so any dependencies are automatically installed and updates can be managed more easily in the future. There are a few steps, but it's pretty straightforward:

Updating the repository sources

1. The first thing we need to do is update our repository sources to include the Webmin repositories:

   ```
   $ sudo nano /etc/apt/sources.list
   ```

2. Add the following two lines to the end of the file:

   ```
   deb http://download.webmin.com/download/repository sarge
   contrib
   ```

```
deb
http://webmin.mirror.somersettechsolutions.co.uk/repository
sarge contrib
```

3. Save and exit Nano.

Importing the signing key

1. Next, we need to download and import the repository's signing key:

   ```
   $ cd ~
   ```

   ```
   $ sudo wget http://www.webmin.com/jcameron-key.asc
   ```

   ```
   $ sudo apt-key add jcameron-key.asc
   ```

2. Now that we have everything we need, we can update the package installer and install Webmin. It can take a while, so you might want to go and make yourself a cup of tea or coffee:

   ```
   $ sudo apt-get update
   ```

   ```
   $ sudo apt-get install webmin
   ```

3. Once it's installed, you should see the following message in the shell window:

Webmin installation

Accessing Webmin locally

Webmin, by default, runs on port 10000 and uses the secure HTTPS protocol; so, to access it, you need to enter the following URL in your browser:

```
https://<my-ip>:10000
```

Where `<my-ip>` is the IP address of your Raspberry Pi.

In the previous chapter, we set up a static IP address on our system; in my case, I set up the address as 192.168.0.99. So, to access Webmin on my system, I would use:

```
https://192.168.0.99:10000
```

HTTPS Privacy Errors

In some browsers, such as Google Chrome, you might see a privacy error as you try to access the Webmin Web page. This is because the SSL certificate behind the HTTPS connection is not signed by a known authority. This is fine—just tell your browser that you want to accept this and proceed (in Chrome, you need to click on the **Advanced** link first to access that option).

You can log into Webmin using the **root** or **pi** user account, or any other account that has **sudo** rights:

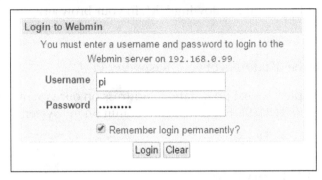

Webmin login

Once logged in, you'll be presented with the main system information page. Have a good poke around in it because there's lots of useful stuff you can see and do.

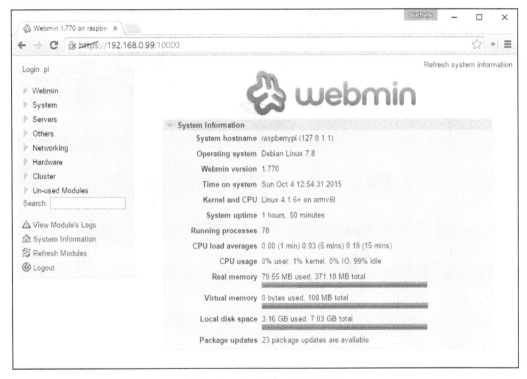

Webmin system information view

Webmin comes with a lot of modules, and not all of them are installed; therefore, you might want to explore the **Un-used Modules** section of the panel to see if there is anything you want to add to Webmin.

Remotely accessing Webmin

In the same way that we set up remote access for our alarm control panel in the previous chapter, you can do it with Webmin—just set up port-forwarding on your router for port 10000. You can then access Webmin from anywhere using `https://<my-public-ip>:10000`.

Summary

Well, this has been a bit of a mix-and-match of various topics to end on before we put together our home security system framework. I hope you enjoyed these various footnotes to previous chapters, and that it's given you some ideas on how far you can take your home security system.

We started by looking at ways we can arm and disarm our system without having to access the Web-based control panel, by adding a mechanical or digital switch to an arm/disarm input.

We then looked at adding analogue-type sensors to our system, which can alert us when a threshold has been reached by using operational amplifiers set up as voltage comparators. The idea behind these comparator circuits can be implemented for different types of sensors where you want to know when a certain voltage threshold has been reached at the analogue sensor output.

Finally, we learned how to install Webmin on our Raspberry Pi so that we can monitor and configure many aspects of the Linux operating system.

The next chapter is the moment we've all been waiting for; we're going to take all of the elements and concepts from the previous chapters and put together our full system comprising the elements we want to feature. The star of the show will be our Bash scripts, which will glue together all of these elements and provide the control logic for the entire system.

Putting It All Together

9

Over the past eight chapters, we've explored the elements and concepts of a full-featured home security system that you'd expect to have installed in your property. It's been presented in a modular fashion so that you can choose which features you want for your system, to allow you to make it as compact and basic or large and complex as you require.

Fundamentally, the idea behind a home security system is to detect whether particular zone inputs are triggered high or low by an external sensor, be that a switch, motion detector, or water detector. At the end of the day, as far as the control software is concerned, the type of sensor is irrelevant and the system software's job is to simply check the state of its inputs and alert accordingly.

In this final chapter, we're going to put all of the concepts together to come up with a security system framework and write the control scripts around it. This is what we will cover:

- Defining a high-level overview of our system, detailing the connected elements
- Building the entire modular security system framework control script, exploring the code in detail
- Delving into some detailed shell scripting techniques to perform certain tasks
- Learning how to make our system automatically start at boot-time
- Preventing the burning out of our SD card by creating a RAM-based file system

Alarm system diagram

So that we don't get lost in this process, the first thing I recommend is to come up with a complete system diagram that we can follow. I do this for any system I design and put together so that it can be built in a structured way, and easily documented and modified.

For the home security system in this chapter, I have come up with the following system diagram that we will look to as a framework. The whole concept is designed to be modular, so you can come up with your own system to suit your requirements and implement it accordingly, using the scripts presented in this chapter.

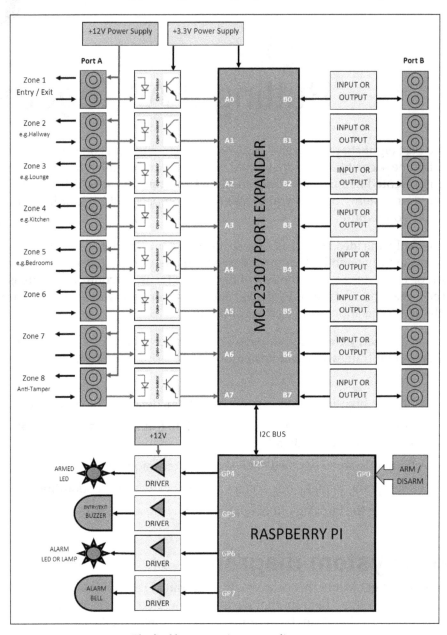

The final home security system diagram

Overview of the system elements

The preceding system diagram comprises the elements and modules that we have discussed in previous chapters. Here's a quick recap of these:

A +12V power supply

This is the primary power supply to our system, which we will obtain from an external mains adapter that could be **battery-backed**. This supply needs to be smooth and regulated to ensure that it remains stable for the system as currently drawn.

All of the alarm wiring and sensors will be supplied with this power, as will peripherals such as sounders and bells, which usually operate from a 12V supply. *Chapter 5, Adding a Passive Infrared Motion Sensor* discussed the merits of using a 12V supply for the alarm circuits.

A +3.3V power supply

This supply is a regulated +3.3V supply for the digital port expander circuit; it also provides the logical alarm zone inputs via an opto-coupler. The +3.3V power supply can be derived from either the +12V supply (recommended), or the +5V supply from the Raspberry Pi's GPIO connector, using a voltage regulator chosen according to how much current you need.

Chapter 3, Extending Your Pi to Connect More Things, showed you how to build a +3.3V regulated supply.

The opto-isolator input module

This will isolate the +12V zone input power lines from the port expander and GPIO digital inputs, which should only have a maximum of +3.3V presented to them when triggered high.

The circuit for these opto-isolated input modules was discussed and shown in *Chapter 5, Adding a Passive Infrared Motion Sensor*.

The port expander

The port expander is our main digital input/output system that will take the alarm zone inputs and transmit them to the Raspberry Pi using the I2C bus, or allow the Raspberry Pi to switch outputs on and off.

We built our MCP23017-based port expander circuit in *Chapter 3, Extending Your Pi to Connect More Things* and configured the software for it in *Chapter 4, Adding a Magnetic Contact Sensor*.

An arm/disarm switch

The arm/disarm input overrides the arm/disarm **soft-switch** function on our web-based control panel, and is a switch (key, digital keypad, or otherwise) connected to GP0 directly on the Raspberry Pi's GPIO connector.

Remember to connect any switch circuit appropriately to the GPIO pin to avoid damage to your Raspberry Pi. This was discussed in *Chapter 2, Connecting Things to Your Pi with GPIO*.

Alarm outputs

In our system, we have several output devices that are controlled by our Raspberry Pi via output driver circuits. We have an output for an entry/exit buzzer, an armed status LED, an alarm bell, and an alarm LED indicator.

These are switched on and off by our Raspberry Pi GPIO connector via driver circuits that allow us to drive high current and inductive loads using the GPIO pins. These driver circuits, based around TIP120 Darlington transistors, were discussed in *Chapter 6, Adding Cameras to Our Security System* and *Chapter 8, A Miscellany of Things*.

Designing the control scripts

Before we start writing the scripts to control our alarm systems, it is probably a good idea to outline the **high-level** process for the system. The following **flow-chart** helps us picture how our system should work, and the various logical decisions our script needs to make.

The flowchart might look a bit complicated with all its lines in different directions, but it's actually pretty linear and in a downward direction. Referring to the flowchart, it shows the following tasks that the control script will be doing:

- Sitting quietly until the system is armed either by the hardware key switch or the web-based panel's soft switch.

- When the system is first armed, it will sound the exit buzzer for a pre-determined amount of time before actually arming the system. This gives you a chance to leave the property or disarm the system again, before it starts monitoring the inputs.

- Once the system is armed, the armed LED will be switched on and the system will wait to see if any of the alarm zone inputs are triggered. It will also wait to see if the alarm is disarmed on your return to the property. We can optionally put an entry timer in here on the entry zone to delay before triggering the alarm.

- If the alarm is ultimately triggered, then the main alarm bell will be switched on, as well as the exit buzzer. The main bell should only sound for a while, depending on environmental restrictions in your neighborhood, and so, this will be switched off after a pre-defined period, but the internal buzzer will stay on.

- When triggered, the system will then wait for you to disarm it, before resetting it.

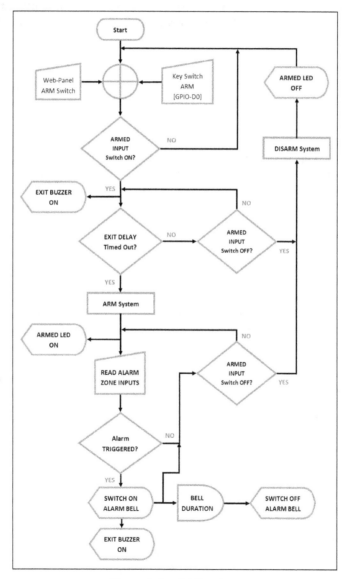

The control script flowchart

Building the control script

Now that we have designed our system the way we want it to work, we can start writing our Bash **control script**. As before, we'll locate our scripts in the folder, /etc/pi-alarm, which, you'll remember from *Chapter 7, Building a Web-Based Control Panel*, is also where our Web-based control panel writes its configuration status file, alarm.cfg to. We'll be referring to that file in our scripts too.

In this script, we are going to use the **bc** tool (the Bash command-line **calculator**) to convert **hex** values to **binary**. It's not installed by default, so you'll need to get the package:

```
$ sudo apt-get update
$ sudo apt-get install bc
```

 Our script file is quite long so, as before, you might want to sit on the sofa and write it on your laptop using something such as Notepad++. Remember, however, if you're using a PC, ensure that the end-of-line (EOL) format is converted to the Unix format, otherwise the Bash script won't run on the Pi when you copy it across. Notepad++ will do this for you.

Exploring the script code

I'm now going to walk you through the various sections of the control script code I've written, which will be used as a framework for our system. I say "framework" because, while it will provide you with a fully functional control script for the system, it can be modified and extended to suit your particular requirements.

The following code listings are all part of the single bash script, alarm-control.sh, that can be downloaded in full with comments from the Packt Publishing website.

Declarations

We'll start off by setting up the various **control variables** needed to track the system's state:

```
#!/bin/bash
#/etc/pi-alarm/alarm-control.sh

ALM_BELL_DURATION=600     #duration in seconds the alarm bell
should sound for
ALM_EXIT_DELAY=30     #entry/exit zone delay in seconds
```

```
ALM_KEY_ARMED=0      #status of the arm/disarm key switch
ALM_SYS_ARMED=0      #armed status of the system

ALM_ZONE_INPUT_READ=""      #this will store the value of the zone
inputs read
ALM_ZONE_INPUT_STAT="00000000"    #binary representation of the inputs
(b7-b0)
ALM_ZONE_INPUT_PREV=""      #previous zone input status
ALM_ZONE_TRIGGER=0    #this will be set to 1 if one or more zones is
triggered
ALM_ZONES_STAT=(0 0 0 0 0 0 0 0)    #dynamic array of normalised zone
status (z1 to z8 order) - 1 is triggered

STAT_RET_VAL=""    #return value from functions
```

Because we could face the situation whereby a HIGH or a LOW input could represent a triggered zone, depending on its configuration and wiring, I have introduced an array of *normalized* status flags in the variable, ALM_ZONES_STAT, which will be the definitive state as far as the script is concerned. We'll look at the function that deals with this later.

Updating config settings

In *Chapter 7*, *Building a Web-Based Control Panel*, we introduced the configuration file, alarm.cfg, which stores the system status and configuration for the benefit of the Web-based control panel. This file not only needs to be read by the main control script to get any settings made using the control panel, but also needs to be updated with status values from the main control script so that they can be presented back to the control panel, essentially exchanging data between the two sub-systems.

Therefore, we're going to include a helper function that contains the same code called by the Web page PHP script to update this file from the control panel:

```
#This helper function will update the alarm config
#file with the specified value (alarm.cfg) so that
#the Web panel can know the latest status
function almUpdateConfigSetting()
{
  #$1 - Setting Name
  #$2 - Setting Value
  sudo sed -i "s/^\($1\s*= *\).*/\1$2/" /etc/pi-alarm/alarm.cfg
}
```

Setting up the GPIO

We now need to set up the Raspberry Pi's GPIO pins for our purposes, as outlined by the earlier system diagram. The following commands were first discussed in *Chapter 2, Connecting Things to Your Pi with GPIO*:

```
# GPIO SET UP ###################################
#Set up the Raspberry Pi GPIO pins
#Refer to Chapter 2 for info
#D0 (GPIO17) Arm/Disarm Key Input
sudo echo 17 > /sys/class/gpio/export
sudo echo in > /sys/class/gpio/gpio17/direction

#D4 (GPIO23) Armed LED Output
sudo echo 23 > /sys/class/gpio/export
sudo echo out > /sys/class/gpio/gpio23/direction
sudo echo 0 > /sys/class/gpio/gpio23/value

#D5 (GPIO24) Exit Buzzer Output
sudo echo 24 > /sys/class/gpio/export
sudo echo out > /sys/class/gpio/gpio24/direction
sudo echo 0 > /sys/class/gpio/gpio24/value

#D6 (GPIO25) Alarm LED Output
sudo echo 25 > /sys/class/gpio/export
sudo echo out > /sys/class/gpio/gpio25/direction
sudo echo 0 > /sys/class/gpio/gpio25/value

#D7 (GPIO4)  Alarm Bell Output
sudo echo 4 > /sys/class/gpio/export
sudo echo out > /sys/class/gpio/gpio4/direction
sudo echo 0 > /sys/class/gpio/gpio4/value
```

 Note that you can only **export** a GPIO pin once, unless it has been subsequently **unexported**. Therefore, you might see the error, echo: write error: Device or resource busy, if you re-run the script when it tries to export the pin again. You can safely ignore this.

We'll also throw in a few helper functions that will easily allow us to switch on or off various outputs to simplify the main code. I'm a big fan of implementing functions, however simple, as they keep the code modular, reusable, and simpler to read in most cases:

```
#This helper function will switch a specified GPIO output on or off
function almSetGPIOValue()
```

```
{
  #$1 - GPIO pin number
  #$2 - Value
  sudo echo $2 > /sys/class/gpio/gpio$1/value
}
#Helper functions to switch on and off the outputs
function almSetArmedLED()
{
  #$1 - 0 or 1 (Off or On)
  almSetGPIOValue 23 $1
  echo "[ALM] Armed LED set to $1"
}
function almSetExitBuzzer()
{
  #$1 - 0 or 1 (Off or On)
  almSetGPIOValue 24 $1
  echo "[ALM] Exit Buzzer set to $1"
}
function almSetAlarmLED()
{
  #$1 - 0 or 1 (Off or On)
  almSetGPIOValue 25 $1
  echo "[ALM] Alarm Trigger LED set to $1"
}
function almSetAlarmBell()
{
  #$1 - 0 or 1 (Off or On)
  almSetGPIOValue 4 $1
  echo "[ALM] Alarm Bell set to $1"
}
```

And, we'll add a helper function that will read the ARM switch status from the D0 (GPIO17) of the Raspberry Pi and from the web-console to see if the ARM soft switch has been set:

```
#this function returns whether the system is armed via
#either the web console or key switch
function almGetArmedSwitchStatus()
{
  STAT_RET_VAL="0"
  #read arm key switch input from
  local L_VAL=$(sudo cat /sys/class/gpio/gpio17/value)
  if [ $L_VAL -eq 1 ]; then
    #system has been armed with key switch
```

```
      echo "[ALM] System ARMED with key switch"
      ALM_KEY_ARMED=1
      almUpdateConfigSetting "SYSTEM_ARMED" "1" #set system armed
        console flag
      STAT_RET_VAL="1"
  else
      #read system armed value from web console config file
      if [ $SYSTEM_ARMED == 1 ]; then
        echo "[ALM] System ARMED with web console"
        STAT_RET_VAL="1"
      fi
  fi
}
```

Setting up the I2C port expander

The next few lines of code set up the I2C port expander to set all of the pins, on both Port A and Port B, as inputs. In our system here, we're only using Port A, but this allows us to have another 8 inputs if we want to expand our system. We originally looked at this in *Chapter 4, Adding a Magnetic Contact Sensor*:

```
# PORT EXPANDER SET UP ##########################
#Refer to Chapter 4 for more information about the I2C bus

#We will set up I/O BUS A as all inputs
sudo i2cset -y 1 0x20 0x00 0xFF

#Whilst we're not using BUS B in our system,
#we can set that up as all inputs too
sudo i2cset -y 1 0x20 0x01 0xFF
```

 If you don't have your I2C port expander attached, then you'll see the following error when you try to run these commands: *Error: Write failed*

Decoding the zone inputs status

The next function is a big one—and key to our system. It will read the Port A value from the I2C port expander. It'll be returned as a hexadecimal value, so we need to convert this to a binary value with a 0 or 1 flag representing each input bit. We'll use the bc tool installed earlier to do this.

Once we have the status of each input bit, we then normalize the status by determining
whether a 0 or a 1 determines a positive trigger. The resulting output is the array,
ALM_ZONES_STAT, which contains the status of each zone—with a 1 representing a
positive triggered zone de-facto:

```
#This function will read the port inputs and set the
#status of each zone
function almReadZoneInputs()
{
  #preserve previous zone status
  ALM_ZONE_INPUT_PREV=$ALM_ZONE_INPUT_STAT
  #read the 8-bit hex value of port a
  ALM_ZONE_INPUT_READ=$(sudo i2cget -y 1 0x20 0x12)

  if [[ $ALM_ZONE_INPUT_READ = *"Error"* ]]; then
    #An error occurred reading the I2C bus - set default value
    ALM_ZONE_INPUT_READ="0x00"
  fi

  #remove the 0x at the start of the value to get the hex value
  local L_HEX=${ALM_ZONE_INPUT_READ:2}
  #convert the hex value to binary
  local L_BIN=$(echo "obase=2; ibase=16; $L_HEX" | bc )
  #zero pad the binary to represent all 8 bits (b7-b0)
  ALM_ZONE_INPUT_STAT=$(printf "%08d" $L_BIN)

  echo "[ALM] Zone I/O Status: $ALM_ZONE_INPUT_STAT
    ($ALM_ZONE_INPUT_READ)"

  #check each zone input to see if it's in a triggered state
  #a triggered state may be either 1 or 0 depending on the input's
    configuration
  #you'll need to set the logic here accordingly for each input
  #the ALM_ZONES_STAT array contains the definitive trigger value
    for each input

  #zone 1 test (bit 0)
  local L_FLG=${ALM_ZONE_INPUT_STAT:7:1}
  if [ $L_FLG -eq 0 ]; then ALM_ZONES_STAT[0]=0; else
    ALM_ZONES_STAT[0]=1; fi

  #zone 2 test (bit 1)
  local L_FLG=${ALM_ZONE_INPUT_STAT:6:1}
  if [ $L_FLG -eq 0 ]; then ALM_ZONES_STAT[1]=0; else
    ALM_ZONES_STAT[1]=1; fi
```

```
#zone 3 test (bit 2)
local L_FLG=${ALM_ZONE_INPUT_STAT:5:1}
if [ $L_FLG -eq 0 ]; then ALM_ZONES_STAT[2]=0; else
  ALM_ZONES_STAT[2]=1; fi

#zone 4 test (bit 3)
local L_FLG=${ALM_ZONE_INPUT_STAT:4:1}
if [ $L_FLG -eq 0 ]; then ALM_ZONES_STAT[3]=0; else
  ALM_ZONES_STAT[3]=1; fi

#zone 5 test (bit 4)
local L_FLG=${ALM_ZONE_INPUT_STAT:3:1}
if [ $L_FLG -eq 0 ]; then ALM_ZONES_STAT[4]=0; else
  ALM_ZONES_STAT[4]=1; fi

#zone 6 test (bit 5)
local L_FLG=${ALM_ZONE_INPUT_STAT:2:1}
if [ $L_FLG -eq 0 ]; then ALM_ZONES_STAT[5]=0; else
  ALM_ZONES_STAT[5]=1; fi

#zone 7 test (bit 6)
local L_FLG=${ALM_ZONE_INPUT_STAT:1:1}
if [ $L_FLG -eq 0 ]; then ALM_ZONES_STAT[6]=0; else
  ALM_ZONES_STAT[6]=1; fi

#zone 8 test (bit 7)
local L_FLG=${ALM_ZONE_INPUT_STAT:0:1}
if [ $L_FLG -eq 0 ]; then ALM_ZONES_STAT[7]=0; else
  ALM_ZONES_STAT[7]=1; fi

echo "[ALM] Zone Trigger Status: $ALM_ZONES_STAT[*]"
}
```

Initialization

Now that we have declared our module-level variables and helper functions, we will start our main routine. First, we'll initialize the system that clears the SYSTEM_ARMED status and reads in the initial settings from the config file:

```
# initialise system #########
echo "[ALM] Initialising system..."
almUpdateConfigSetting "SYSTEM_ARMED" "0" #clear system armed
console flag
sleep 1
sudo cat /etc/pi-alarm/alarm.cfg
```

```
sleep 1
echo "[ALM] Initialising done"
#############################
```

The system monitoring loop

The script then jumps into a never-ending loop that will be the main control system, monitoring the arm/disarm status and, when armed, monitoring the zone input status and responding accordingly:

```
# loop continuously###########
while true
do

    # wait for system to be armed ##############
    echo "[ALM] Alarm now in STAND-BY state - waiting to be armed"
    almSetArmedLED 0 #switch off armed LED
    STAT_RET_VAL="0"
    while [[ $STAT_RET_VAL = "0" ]]; do
      sleep 1
      #read the control panel status file
      . /etc/pi-alarm/alarm.cfg
      almGetArmedSwitchStatus #result is returned in STAT_RET_VAL
      echo -n "*" # indicate standby mode
    done
    ############################################
```

Arming the system

When the system goes into the ARMED state, it will first switch on the exit buzzer and then wait for a pre-determined amount of time. This will give you time to leave the property or disarm the system:

```
# perform exit delay #####################
echo "[ALM] Alarm now in EXIT DELAY state"
almSetExitBuzzer 1 #switch on exit buzzer
COUNTER=$ALM_EXIT_DELAY
while [[ $STAT_RET_VAL = "1" && $COUNTER -gt 0 ]]; do
  sleep 1
  #read the control panel status file
  . /etc/pi-alarm/alarm.cfg
  almGetArmedSwitchStatus #result is returned in STAT_RET_VAL
  COUNTER-=1
  echo -n "X$COUNTER " # indicate exit mode
```

```
done
almSetExitBuzzer 0 #switch off exit buzzer
############################################

# system now armed - monitor inputs #########
ALM_SYS_ARMED=1
echo "[ALM] Alarm now in ARMED state"
almSetArmedLED 1 #switch on armed LED

#read the control panel status file
. /etc/pi-alarm/alarm.cfg
almReadZoneInputs  # > ALM_ZONES_STAT[x]
```

Monitoring the zones

Once armed, the system will monitor the zone inputs in a continuous loop until either the system is disarmed, or a zone input is triggered. When a zone is triggered, it will check against the ZONE_ENABLE_n configuration to see if that zone has been disabled (this is done in the Web-based control panel). If the zone is not disabled, then the alarm system is deemed triggered.

The ZONE_STATUS_n setting is also updated here so that the web-based control panel indicates which zone or zones have been triggered:

```
#check each zone input to set if it's enable
#and has been triggered
#NUM_ZONES setting is stored in alarm.cfg

while [[ $ALM_SYS_ARMED -eq 1 ]]; do
  echo -n "A" #indicate armed mode

  ALM_ZONE_TRIGGER=0
  for (( i=$NUM_ZONES; i>0; i-- )); do
    if [[ $ALM_ZONES_STAT[$i-1] -eq 1 ]]; then
      #zone has been triggered
      echo "[ALM] Zone $i TRIGGERED"
      E_VAR="ZONE_ENABLE_$i"
      E_VAL=`echo "$E_VAR"` #get zone enabled status loaded from
        alarm.cfg

      if [[ $E_VAL -eq 1 ]]; then
        #zone is enabled
        ALM_ZONE_TRIGGER=1 #set alarm triggered flag
        echo "[ALM] Zone $i ENABLED - alarm will be triggered"
```

```
          almUpdateConfigSetting "ZONE_STATUS_$i" "1"

          ## YOU CAN INSERT CODE HERE TO TAKE CAMERA IMAGE IF YOU
             WANT##
          ## REFER BACK TO CHAPTER 6 ##


     fi
   fi
done


. /etc/pi-alarm/alarm.cfg
almGetArmedSwitchStatus #result is returned in STAT_RET_VAL
```

Entry delay

When an alarm zone is triggered, it will first check whether it was the entry/exit zone that was triggered. If it was, then the system will delay before sounding the main alarm to give you a chance to disarm the system. Only the entry buzzer will sound at this time:

```
if [[ $ALM_ZONE_TRIGGER -eq 1 ]]; then
   # alarm has been triggered
   almSetAlarmLED 1
   echo "[ALM] A zone has been triggered"

   ###################################
   # ZONE 1 is the ENTRY zone - if that's triggered then delay
   if [[ $ALM_ZONES_STAT[0] -eq 1 ]]; then
     # perform entry delay ##########
     echo "[ALM] Alarm now in ENTRY state"
     setExitBuzzer 1 #switch on entry/exit buzzer

     COUNTER=$ALM_EXIT_DELAY
     STAT_RET_VAL="0"
     while [[ $STAT_RET_VAL = "1" && $COUNTER -gt 0 ]]; do
       echo -n "E$COUNTER " #indicate entry mode
       sleep 1
       #read the control panel status file
       . /etc/pi-alarm/alarm.cfg
       almGetArmedSwitchStatus #result is returned in STAT_RET_VAL
       COUNTER-=1
     done
   fi
   ###################################
```

Sounding the main alarm

If, at this point, the system hasn't been disarmed, then we need to sound the main bell. We have a duration limit for sounding the bell to cater to environmental noise restrictions; we wouldn't want the alarm sounding for hours, annoying the neighbors until we got home. At this point, you can also add code from *Chapter 6, Adding Cameras to Our Security System*, if you want to be sent an alert email to your mobile device:

```
#####################################
# STAY in TRIGGERED mode until system has been disarmed
if [[ $STAT_RET_VAL = "1" ]]; then
  #alarm has not been disabled
  almSetAlarmBell 1 #switch on alarm bell
  echo "[ALM] Alarm now in TRIGGERED state"

  ## YOU CAN INSERT CODE HERE TO SEND YOU AN EMAIL IF YOU
    WANT##
  ## REFER BACK TO CHAPTER 6 ##

  COUNTER=0
  STAT_RET_VAL="0"
  while [[ $STAT_RET_VAL = "1" ]]; do
    echo -n "T$COUNTER " #indicate triggered mode
    sleep 1
    #read the control panel status file
    . /etc/pi-alarm/alarm.cfg
    almGetArmedSwitchStatus #result is returned in STAT_RET_VAL

    COUNTER+=1
    if [[ $COUNTER -gt $ALM_BELL_DURATION ]]; then
      almSetAlarmBell 0 #switch off alarm bell
      echo "[ALM] Bell has been switched OFF"
    fi
  done
fi
#####################################
```

Disarming and resetting the system

When we disarm the system, we need to reset its status and complete the monitoring loop so that we can start all over again and wait for it to be re-armed:

```
# alarm has been disarmed #########
echo "[ALM] Alarm has been DISARMED"
```

```
    ALM_SYS_ARMED=0
    almSetAlarmBell 0 #switch off alarm bell
    almSetExitBuzzer 0 #switch off exit buzzer
    almSetAlarmLED 0
    almSetArmedLED 0 #switch off armed LED


    ###################################
  fi

  done
  ###########################################

done
#############################################
```

We're done (almost)...

And there we have it: a framework for an entire alarm control script on our Raspberry Pi. Additional features that you may want to implement within your script could include the following:

- Sending a photo or video clip from a zone's camera when it's triggered
- Sending an email alert with status details when the alarm has been triggered
- Writing a regular log file recording historical status information
- Adding additional environmental sensors to port B

 Each of the script blocks is taken from the single script file, alarm-control.sh, so you should be able to put all of the described pieces together into one file to have a fully functional script.

As always, before we can run it we need to give the script execute rights:

```
$ sudo chmod 777 /etc/pi-alarm/alarm-control.sh
```

After we copy the script to our Raspberry Pi, this is what we should see in our /etc/pi-alarm folder:

```
pi@raspberrypi ~ $ ls -1 /etc/pi-alarm
alarm.cfg
alarm-control.sh
update-alarm-setting.sh
```

Automatically starting the system

Now, obviously, we don't want to have to manually start the alarm control script each time the Raspberry Pi boots up, for example, after a power failure—for a start, we may not even be there. Therefore, we need to set up our operating system so that it will automatically start up the `alarm-control.sh` script at boot time.

To do this, we need to edit the `rc.local` file using Nano:

```
$ sudo nano /etc/rc.local
```

Before the line containing `exit 0`, insert the following line:

```
sudo /etc/pi-alarm/alarm-control.sh &
```

> The & symbol at the end of the line is important because it will then make the script run in a different process, otherwise the `rc.local` script would never exit.

Your `rc.local` file should now look something like this:

```
#!/bin/sh -e
#
# rc.local
#
# This script is executed at the end of each multiuser runlevel.
# Make sure that the script will "exit 0" on success or any other
# value on error.
#
# In order to enable or disable this script just change the execution
# bits.
#
# By default this script does nothing.

# Print the IP address
_IP=$(hostname -I) || true
if [ "$_IP" ]; then
  printf "My IP address is %s\n" "$_IP"
fi

sudo /etc/pi-alarm/alarm-control.sh &
exit 0
```

The operating system runs the `rc.local` script after the system boots up, so you can put anything in there that you want to happen automatically at this time.

Preserving the SD card

One final topic I want to share with you is that of preserving your Raspberry Pi's SD card. SD cards have a finite write cycle, and continuous writing to the card will eventually burn it out. If we're going to be writing lots of log file entries and taking lots of camera images, we will want to protect our SD card in order to maintain the integrity and reliability of our system; using the system RAM instead can help us with this.

Creating a RAM-based file system

Our Raspberry Pi has plenty of fast system RAM available to us (1Gb on the latest models) that isn't susceptible to this write burn-out issue. Therefore, I'm going to show you how to allocate some of it to create a temporary disk in memory, which we can write files to that we don't need kept on the SD card. Such files would include the, quite large, camera image files that will be emailed out of the system— which, therefore, don't need to be stored permanently. You should also consider any log files that are regularly written to, which would then be shipped off the system at regular intervals.

 Remember that this is a RAM-based file system, so content will be lost when the Raspberry Pi shuts down or reboots. So, don't store any data here that you want to persist after a restart.

Let's create a Bash script file called setup-ramfs.sh, and copy it to our /etc/pi-alarm folder:

```
#!/bin/bash
#/etc/pi-alarm/setup-ramfs.sh

RAM_DISK="/ramfs"
RAM_DISK_SIZE=64M

# Create RAM Disk #######################
if [ ! -z "$RAM_DISK" ]; then
  echo "[INIT] Creating RAM Disk... $RAM_DISK"
  mkdir -p $RAM_DISK
  chmod 777 $RAM_DISK
  mount -t tmpfs -o size=$RAM_DISK_SIZE tmpts $RAM_DISK/
  echo "[INIT] RAM Disk created at $RAM_DISK"
fi
##############################################
```

`setup-ramfs.sh` RAM disk creation script

Running the preceding script will create a RAM disk folder at `/ramfs`—you can treat it just like any other folder; it's just that it resides in the system memory rather than on the SD card:

```
$ cd /ramfs
$ ls
```

You can call this script from the `alarm-control.sh` script as part of the initialization process by including the line:

```
. /etc/pi-alarm/setup-ramfs.sh
```

Conclusion

The Raspberry Pi is a powerful little beast and a great platform for building low-cost, but highly capable, embedded systems. The interfaces built into its GPIO connector make it easy to bolt on modules using simple low-cost electronics and a bit of configuration to create very functional and flexible systems. The inclusion of a dedicated camera interface and networking interfaces give you everything you could possible need for an Internet-connected home security system.

I've covered a lot of topics in this book, and I could have gone on and on, but I hope that what I have presented has been done in a structured and methodical way, and has given you the tools and techniques to carry on this journey so that you are able to create the perfect home security system for your needs.

Tips for building systems

As a systems guy who has to work with many different technologies and disciplines on a day-to-day basis, I just want to leave you with the following thoughts to consider, if you choose to build upon the system we've put together in this book, which, of course, I hope you will:

- Create a high-level diagram of your proposed system first—a bit like the one I produced earlier in this chapter.

- Define everything in a modular way so that you can build and test your system in small chunks. This makes it much easier to spot issues early on.

- Building the system using smaller modules makes it easier to re-use and replace circuits and code, and don't be afraid to mix-and-match technologies using what's best for the individual module.

- Don't try to re-invent the wheel — use existing code and circuit resources that are proven to work. This makes it much quicker to get things working and minimizes the number of times you have to hit your head against a brick wall. I call it blagging.

Summary

Well, we've reached the end of our journey to build a fully functional and extensible home security system using the mighty Raspberry Pi mini-PC. In this final chapter, we put together all of the elements and concepts from the previous chapters to create a home security framework, both from a hardware and software perspective.

In particular, this chapter guided us toward building a modular framework for our home security system, implementing features that you would find in any commercially available system, and also things that you don't see out there. We walked through the complete control script, exploring its various sections and understanding how they fit into our system.

We also learned how to automatically start-up our home security system script when our Raspberry Pi boots up, and how data is shared between the Pi and the web-based control panel in real-time via the configuration file. Finally, we looked at how to prevent our SD card from burning out by creating a rather useful RAM-based temporary file system.

Index

T

TIP120 Darlington transistor 93

U

**Universal Asynchronous Receiver and
Transmitter (UART) bus 22**
Universal Serial Bus (USB) ports 22, 23
USB webcam
  about 97
  fswebcam, setting up 98
  installing 97
  snap, capturing 98
  URL 97
  using 97

V

video
  capturing 87, 88
  using, in security system 88
visudo utility 118

W

Webmin
  about 135
  accessing locally 137-139
  pi user 138
  remotely accessing 139
  repository sources, updating 135
  root user account 138
  signing key, importing 136
  URL 135, 139

web page
  control panel HTML template 108
  creating 108
  main PHP code 118
  modifying dynamically 117
  PHP configuration file setting,
    modifying 117
  running, as different user 118, 119
  styling 109, 116
web server
  installing 102
  PHP5 installation, testing 103, 104
Wi-Fi
  Raspberry Pi, connecting via 17
Win32 Disk Imager utility
  URL 7
**wireless motion sensors (wireless
    PIR sensors)**
  433-MHz receiver, connecting 74, 75
  433-MHz wireless alarm systems 73
  about 73
  receiver wiring diagram 77

Z

zones
  creating 62

Thank you for buying
Building a Home Security System with Raspberry Pi

About Packt Publishing

Packt, pronounced 'packed', published its first book, *Mastering phpMyAdmin for Effective MySQL Management*, in April 2004, and subsequently continued to specialize in publishing highly focused books on specific technologies and solutions.

Our books and publications share the experiences of your fellow IT professionals in adapting and customizing today's systems, applications, and frameworks. Our solution-based books give you the knowledge and power to customize the software and technologies you're using to get the job done. Packt books are more specific and less general than the IT books you have seen in the past. Our unique business model allows us to bring you more focused information, giving you more of what you need to know, and less of what you don't.

Packt is a modern yet unique publishing company that focuses on producing quality, cutting-edge books for communities of developers, administrators, and newbies alike. For more information, please visit our website at www.packtpub.com.

About Packt Open Source

In 2010, Packt launched two new brands, Packt Open Source and Packt Enterprise, in order to continue its focus on specialization. This book is part of the Packt Open Source brand, home to books published on software built around open source licenses, and offering information to anybody from advanced developers to budding web designers. The Open Source brand also runs Packt's Open Source Royalty Scheme, by which Packt gives a royalty to each open source project about whose software a book is sold.

Writing for Packt

We welcome all inquiries from people who are interested in authoring. Book proposals should be sent to author@packtpub.com. If your book idea is still at an early stage and you would like to discuss it first before writing a formal book proposal, then please contact us; one of our commissioning editors will get in touch with you.

We're not just looking for published authors; if you have strong technical skills but no writing experience, our experienced editors can help you develop a writing career, or simply get some additional reward for your expertise.

Learning Raspberry Pi

ISBN: 978-1-78398-282-0   Paperback: 258 pages

Unlock your creative programming potential by creating web technologies, image processing, electronics- and robotics-based projects using the Raspberry Pi

1. Learn how to create games, web, and desktop applications using the best features of the Raspberry Pi.

2. Discover the powerful development tools that allow you to cross-compile your software and build your own Linux distribution for maximum performance.

3. Step-by-step tutorials show you how to quickly develop real-world applications using the Raspberry Pi.

Raspberry Pi Cookbook for Python Programmers

ISBN: 978-1-84969-662-3   Paperback: 402 pages

Over 50 easy-to-comprehended tailor-made recipes to get the most out of the Raspberry Pi and unleash its huge potential using Python

1. Install your first operating system, share files over the network, and run programs remotely.

2. Unleash the hidden potential of the Raspberry Pi's powerful Video Core IV graphics processor with your own hardware accelerated 3D graphics.

3. Discover how to create your own electronic circuits to interact with the Raspberry Pi.

Please check **www.PacktPub.com** for information on our titles

Raspberry Pi Robotic Projects

ISBN: 978-1-84969-432-2   Paperback: 278 pages

Create amazing robotic projects on a shoestring budget

1. Make your projects talk and understand speech with Raspberry Pi.

2. Use standard webcam to make your projects see and enhance vision capabilities.

3. Full of simple, easy-to-understand instructions to bring your Raspberry Pi online for developing robotics projects.

Raspberry Pi Server Essentials

ISBN: 978-1-78328-469-6   Paperback: 116 pages

Transform your Raspberry Pi into a server for hosting websites, games, or even your Bitcoin network

1. Unlock the various possibilities of using Raspberry Pi as a server.

2. Configure a media center for your home or sharing with friends.

3. Connect to the Bitcoin network and manage your wallet.

Please check **www.PacktPub.com** for information on our titles